V ... A Day
F ... ving?

Hidden inside you is a joy of life... waiting to be released! Yoga is the key to this inner beauty of body and mind. Discover a lasting serenity and strength in just minutes a day... at your own pace... in your own spare time!

Richard Hittleman has aimed this remarkable new masterwork at busy people like you... who are interested, curious about Yoga, but without the time or energy for long, arduous exercise plans. He has condensed the essence of Yoga into graduated, short sessions you can manage easily and enjoyably from the moment you begin.

Hundreds of beautiful photos... step-by-step movements... techniques for special problems... all help you learn the Yoga classics that have brought spiritual and physical fulfillment to millions.

Day by day, you'll find yourself growing slimmer, stronger, more graceful. Physical discomforts will vanish. Peace of mind will replace anxiety. . You'll look, act and feel more truly alive!

Bantam Books by Richard Hittleman
Ask your bookseller for the books you have missed

RICHARD HITTLEMAN'S GUIDE TO YOGA MEDITATION
RICHARD HITTLEMAN'S INTRODUCTION TO YOGA
RICHARD HITTLEMAN'S YOGA FOR TOTAL FITNESS
WEIGHT CONTROL THROUGH YOGA
YOGA 28 DAY EXERCISE BOOK

RICHARD
HITTLEMAN'S

INTRODUCTION TO YOGA

BANTAM BOOKS
TORONTO · NEW YORK · LONDON · SYDNEY

RICHARD HITTLEMAN'S INTRODUCTION TO YOGA
A Bantam Book / published by arrangement with Workman Publishing Company, Inc.

Bantam edition / August 1969

2nd printing .... November 1970
3rd printing .... May 1971
4th printing ..... September 1971
5th printing ...... February 1972
6th printing .... June 1972
7th printing ..... November 1972
8th printing .... July 1973
9th printing .... July 1974
10th printing ...... October 1974
11th printing .... June 1975
12th printing .... March 1976
13th printing .... June 1976
14th printing .... July 1977
15th printing .... May 1978
16th printing .... September 1979
17th printing .... November 1979
18th printing .... December 1980

Cover and Inside Photographs by Al Weber

ISBN 0-553-14771-4

Published simultaneously in the United States and Canada

Bantam Books are published by Bantam Books, Inc. Its trademark, consisting of the words "Bantam Books" and the portrayal of a bantam, is Registered in U.S. Patent and Trademark Office and in other countries. Marca Registrada. Bantam Books, Inc., 666 Fifth Avenue, New York, New York 10103.

PRINTED IN THE UNITED STATES OF AMERICA

27 26 25 24 23 22 21 20

CONTENTS

To Mort

PREFACE

There are hundreds of thousands of Americans of all ages and with all physical backgrounds who are now practicing Yoga on a daily basis. They have discovered that not only does Yoga provide the most practical approach to attaining a high level of physical fitness, but it stabilizes the emotions and elevates one's mental attitude. *It is a wholistic approach to the well-being of the entire organism.*

The various systems of Yoga date from dim antiquity. They were designed, and have been practiced throughout the centuries, for the purpose of cultivating human potential. The ancient *gurus* (masters) were deeply aware that each aspect of man's existence, physical, mental, spiritual, was capable of extensive development and they proposed that the main objective of life should be the serious undertaking of this development—that true peace and happiness lay in discovering one's true self and that the science of Yoga would provide a path to "self-realization"; toward this end a number of different types of Yoga were evolved. *Hatha* Yoga, the subject of this book, is concerned primarily with the *physical* aspect of our being; it is comprised of a series of ingenious body attitudes (postures, *asanas*) and certain breathing exercises.

Having introduced and taught Hatha Yoga to several million Americans, I have had ample opportunity to carefully observe that the most successful learning process is one of very gradual assimilation. As such, the profound Yoga movements *must be introduced to the organism in graduated stages.* Many people who subsequently became my students had formerly been discouraged from undertaking the Yoga study through books, magazines, newspapers or demonstrations in which only advanced positions of the postures were depicted—positions that actually require weeks or months of progressive practice to attain. The impression that these people received was: If you can't perform a completed Head Stand or a Full-Lotus *now,* it is useless to consider the practice of Yoga. This is a most unfortunate conclusion and I therefore find it essential to convey to the prospective student that the Hatha Yoga program is begun by his assuming only the most elementary positions — those that can usually be accomplished by anyone who is capable of normal movement, and that if he allows his body to "set" itself in these, as instructed, he can certainly progress to the more advanced work. Also, he must realize that, in the beginning stages, the benefits of the elementary positions are just as great as those of the advanced.

This book offers the necessary *graduated* program. It contains the same progressive concept of instruction that I employ in my classes and *Yoga For Health* television programs. There are two sections, Elementary and Intermediate, and these enable you to derive maximum benefits from each posture while progressing according to your individual ability.

How To Use The Book

Each day, perform as many of the exercises from the Elementary Section as your time permits. Follow all directions to the letter. You need not attempt to perfect the postures, simply *do* them. In this manner, work through the entire Elementary Section. Upon completion, turn to the "Intermediate Section," page 125. The text will explain how to include the intermediate positions in your practice. When you understand this, refer to the "Daily Practice Routines," page 187. These routines will enable you to begin a methodical plan of practice.

If you wish to deal with a particular physical problem, consult the "Special Problems Index," page 189, upon your completion of the Elementary Section.

Regarding Practice

- Select a well-ventilated area where distractions are at a minimum. The Yoga movements require a flat surface and sufficient space to stretch your trunk and limbs without interference.
- Cover your practice surface with a large towel, mat or pad. This cover is put away after exercising and kept only for Yoga practice.
- Your exercise clothing should allow for complete freedom of movement. Most women prefer leotards. Remove watch, eyeglasses and all confining apparel. Keep watch or clock handy for the timing of certain exercises.
- You can practice before eating (stomach empty) but wait at least 90 minutes following meals.
- If in doubt regarding the effect of the Yoga tech-

niques, or if you are currently receiving medical attention, consult your physician before proceeding.

Twenty years of the practice and teaching of Hatha Yoga are reduced to their essence in this book. From extensive experience I do not hesitate to state that if you will patiently follow the instructions herein you will soon note a wonderful, positive change in all aspects of your life.

Richard L. Hittleman
Carmel, California

ELEMENTARY SECTION

1 / DEEP RELAXATION POSTURE
(Salvasana)

OBJECTIVE OF THE DEEP RELAXATION POSTURE

To achieve deep relaxation of body and mind.

If you have thought of Yoga as a form of calisthenics, you will be surprised to learn that our first technique, depicted in Fig. 1, requires absolutely no movement at all! Indeed, the more passive, quiet and motionless one can become, the more the benefits that are derived from this "exercise."

Hatha Yoga represents a radical departure from those systems of body conditioning that stress quick, forceful, repetitive muscular movement to attain physical fitness. Yogic theory suggests to us that a program for cultivating true fitness of the organism must include not only exercises for *all* of the systems of the body, i.e., nervous, endocrine, respiratory, etc., but techniques for the health and stability of the mind and emotions. In other words, any plan that purports to promote genuine physical fitness and to cultivate the body's untapped resources must consider *the entire organism as a unified whole.* This is true regardless of a person's age or physical condition. To the Yogi, weight lifting, isometrics, jogging, certain sports, the use of various machines for body conditioning or figure improvement and the usual "setting-up" exercises with their huffing, puffing and general exertion are all highly questionable, especially from the viewpoint of *overall* physical and mental fitness. Yoga proposes that the health of the organism requires a total, not a fragmented approach; you will experience how ingeniously this theme is developed as you progress in the postures. ("Posture" is generally more descriptive of the Yoga movements than "exercise," although both words are used.)

We begin with the Deep Relaxation Posture, not only because it is an excellent technique to prepare the body for the profound, slow motion movements that follow, but because it frees the mind from its worries and innumerable distractions and allows it to focus fully on what is being done. The benefits of Yoga are greatly increased when the consciousness is fixed on the movements and not allowed to wander.

Deep relaxation is a duet of the body and mind in repose, a passive state wherein there is a renewal of the life-force. This Posture provides the technique that will eventually enable you to achieve complete relaxation whenever you wish, even in the midst of your activities.

FIG. 1 — *Lie on your back and close your eyes. Allow the body to go limp and adjust arms and legs as they feel more comfortable.*

Now, direct your attention into your legs and become aware of your feet. Make certain they are not tensed.

Next, become aware of your ankles and calves and, again, all muscles in these areas should be consciously relaxed.

In a similar manner slowly direct your attention to each area of the body in turn: thighs, abdomen, chest; then hands, arms and shoulders; then neck; finally, the face and head. Become acutely aware of total relaxation in each of these areas. When your attention reaches the head area, your entire organism will be in a state of deep relaxation.

Remain in this state for approximately thirty seconds (or longer if necessary) and then slowly begin your Yoga exercises.

Important

Keep your attention fixed on what you are doing. If you find your mind is wandering, bring it back, gently but firmly, to that point of the body from where it was distracted. In the beginning frequent distractions may occur, but patient practice will result in unswerving concentration.

Practice Information

Perform the Posture to begin each practice session or at any time of the day when deep relaxation is required.

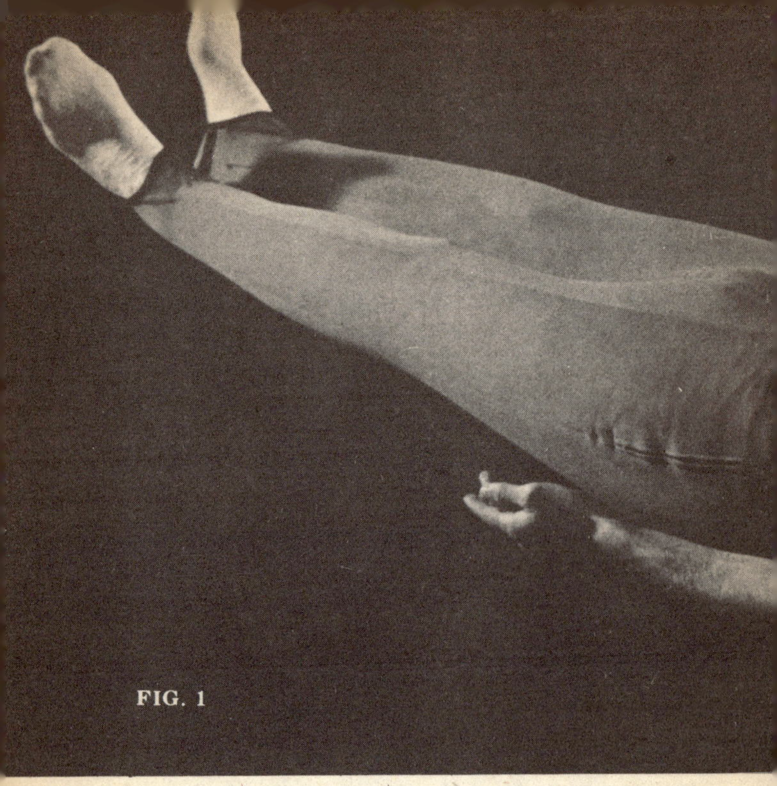

FIG. 1

2 / LOTUS *(Sukhasana; Siddhasana)*

OBJECTIVES OF THE LOTUS POSTURES:
To achieve flexibility of the knees, ankles and feet; to be able to remain firmly seated for several minutes without movement.

To the uninformed, these cross-legged positions often appear as parlor tricks or feats exhibited by those who are double-jointed. However, the Yoga student is well aware that the Lotus postures not only provide an excellent opportunity to remove stiffness and tension from the knees, legs and feet but, of greater interest, afford a man-

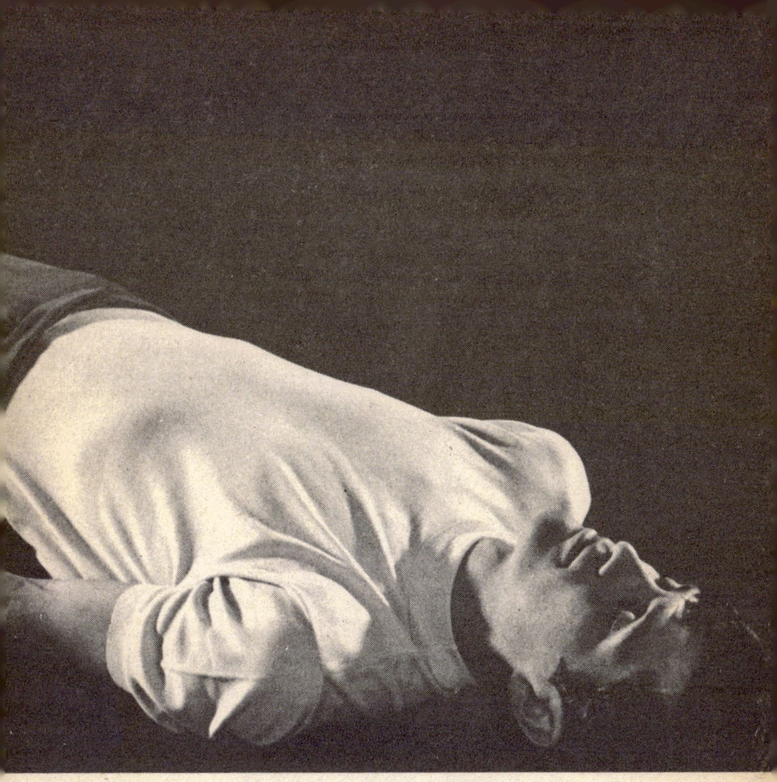

ner of sitting in which certain profound breathing and meditation exercises can be undertaken to excellent advantage.

The great Yogis of ancient India observed that the vitally important practice of meditation (deep introspection) was best accomplished by assuming a posture in which the spine could be held erect (the psychic energies contained in the channels of the spine must be able to flow freely between the base of the spine and the brain); the legs placed in a position that would not require their frequent movement (when the consciousness is focused upon a fixed point, it must not be distracted through any movement whatsoever); and in which the trunk and head could be held steady for extended intervals (the elevated state that is experienced during meditation often makes a longer sitting period highly desirable). The various Lotus postures evolved from these requirements.

Since a number of our exercises and breathing techniques are performed in a seated position, two of the cross-legged postures are introduced at this early point of our study. This will give you an opportunity to gradually acquire the flexibility of the knees, ankles and feet that is necessary for the Half and Full-Lotus.

Important

It is surprising how quickly your legs can adjust to these positions. If you attempt the Half-Lotus for approximately two minutes each day, first with the right foot on top and then with the legs reversed, you should note definite progress within two weeks. If your knee is uncom-

FIG. 2

fortably high or your ankles sustain too much pressure, revert to the simple posture of Fig. 2 for the present.

Practice Information

Sit in one of these three positions whenever a "cross-legged" posture is indicated for subsequent exercises.

FIG. 2 — *This is the simple cross-legged posture that will be adequate for those who find the Half-Lotus too difficult at this time.*

The ankles are crossed in front of you and drawn in as far as possible. Your trunk is erect, eyelids lowered (not closed) and hands rest on knees.

FIG. 3 — *Your hands place the left foot as illustrated. The heel has been drawn in as far as possible and the left foot rests* against, *not under, the right thigh.*

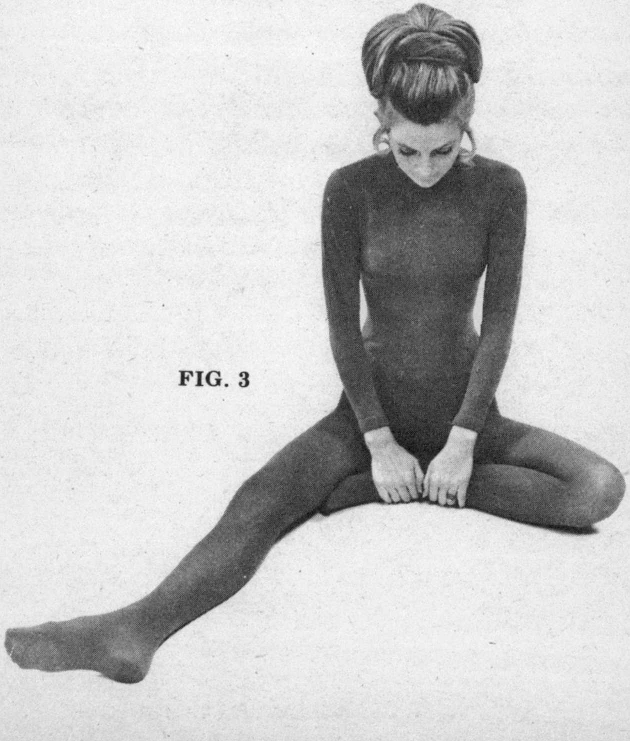

FIG. 3

FIG. 4

FIG. 4 — *The completed Half-Lotus. The right foot can be placed on top of the left thigh or, if you prefer, in the cleft of the left leg.*

Attempt the same position with the legs reversed.

3 / COMPLETE BREATH *(Pranayama)*

OBJECTIVE OF THE COMPLETE BREATH:

To completely fill the lungs with air in a slow, controlled, rhythmic manner.

The element that sustains life is known in the Yogic system as *prana;* this may be translated as "life-force." The primary source of life-force is found in the air; therefore, *how* we breathe has a more immediate and pronounced effect on our existence than any other physical function! The relationship between our health and the manner in which we are breathing is so direct that it is frequently overlooked in its obviousness. If you are lacking in vitality, if your circulation or complexion is poor, if you are tense, nervous, easily upset and subject to frequent headaches, if your thinking is negative and your mind continually disturbed, the Yogi will suggest that the first function to be examined is your breathing. Partial, shallow, erratic or mouth breathing are a few of the faulty types of respiration that may be responsible for more ills than we can enumerate.

The Yogis, perhaps more than any other group, have been involved in a painstakingly detailed investigation of both the various types of breathing that are possible and the effects that these have had on the entire organism. This investigation has extended over many centuries and the findings are so fascinating and significant that they must be very carefully considered by everyone who is interested not only in maintaining a high level of health but *in awakening and utilizing certain powerful forces that lie dormant within the organism.*

The aspect of these findings that will concern us in this book is: The more *complete and rhythmic* the breathing, the more life-force that will be available to the individual. I am well aware from my experience with many thousands of Yoga students that increased life-force can make an enormous difference in every aspect of one's existence. Therefore, the Complete Breath is offered at this point so that the reader may, within a very short period of time, experience for himself the wonderful sense of exhilaration and well-being that can result from this technique. Also, it is important to note that in more advanced Yoga complete breathing and breath control play a vital role.

It is erroneous to equate the phrase "complete breathing" with "deep breathing." You can breathe "deeply" and still not fill the lungs completely. Because *complete* breathing, in a rhythmic fashion, is of such great importance, we must carefully learn and practice the method of its execution.

Important

All breathing is very slow and very quiet. Practice to make the movements *flow* into one another. Eyes can be closed.

Practice Information

Perform 5 times. Practice whenever necessary to revitalize, relieve tension and headaches, clear the mind. Also helps to decrease the cigarette habit.

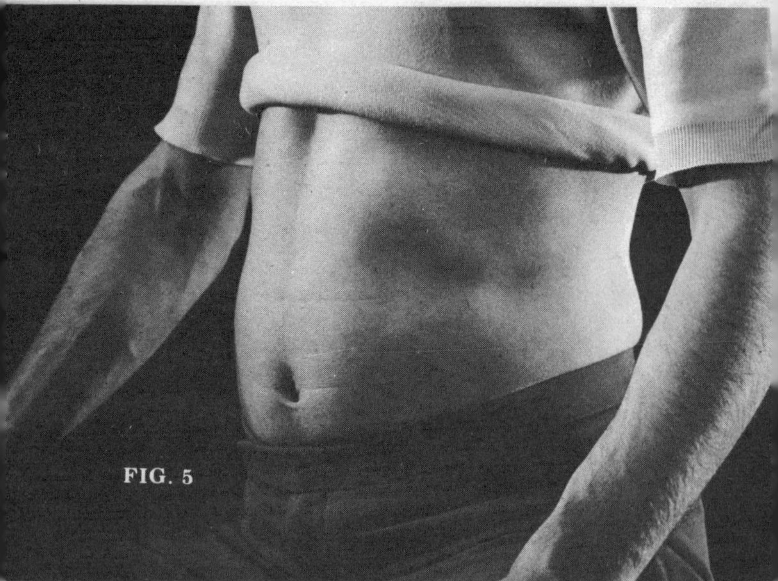

FIG. 5

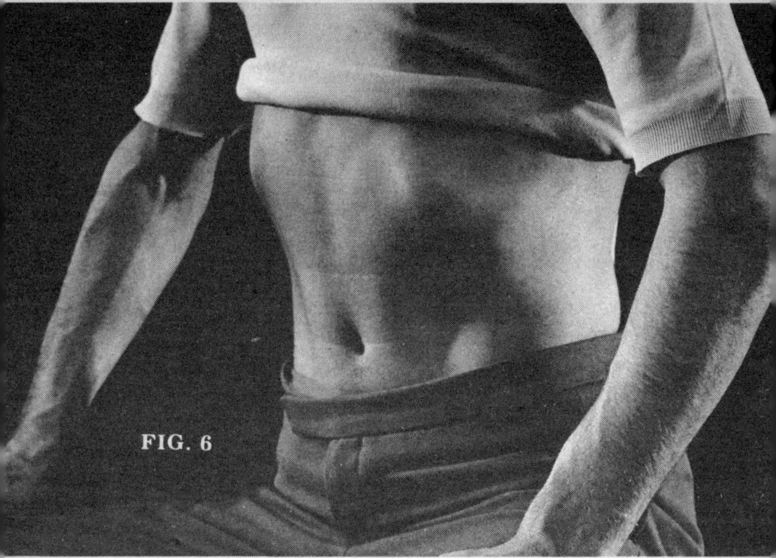

FIG. 6

This exercise is best accomplished in three stages: abdomen, chest and shoulders.

FIG. 5—*Sit in any one of the cross-legged postures you have found comfortable. Exercise the abdominal muscles so as to gain some control of them. First, use these muscles to distend (push out) the abdomen, then contract. Practice these movements until the distensions and contractions are definite.*

Now begin a slow exhalation through your nose (all breathing is done through the nose); simultaneously contract your abdomen until the lungs are completely emptied.

Begin a very slow inhalation and simultaneously distend the abdomen (this allows the air to enter the lower area of the lungs).

FIG. 6—Continue the slow inhalation. *Contract the abdomen slightly and simultaneously expand your chest as much as possible.*

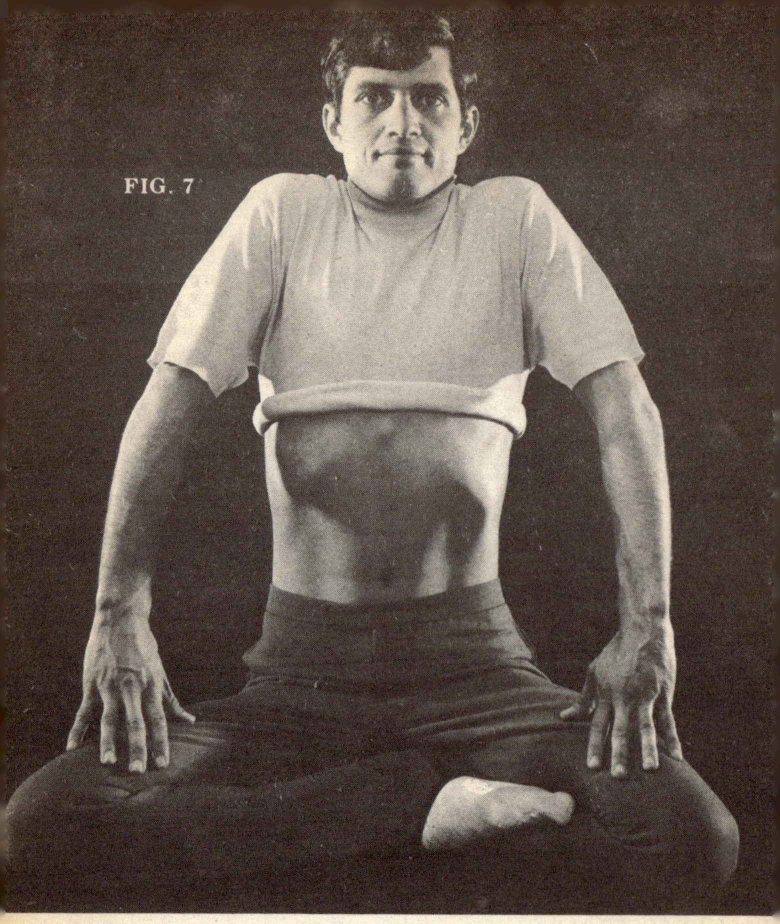

FIG. 7

FIG. 7—Continue the slow inhalation. *Slowly raise your shoulders as high as possible. This movement allows the air to enter the high area of the lungs.*

Retain the breath with your shoulders raised for a count of 5.

Very slowly execute a deep exhalation. Simultaneously allow your body to relax; contract the abdomen and without pause, repeat the three movements.

4 / BACK STRETCH
(Paschimottanasana)

OBJECTIVES OF THE BACK STRETCH:
To remove tension, promote flexibility, strengthen, release trapped energy.

An important objective of our Yoga study is to remove tension while simultaneously strengthening and developing every area of the body. The back and spine receive particular attention in this procedure, first, because the back is so easily subject to a multitude of aches, pains and discomforts, and secondly, because there is great energy trapped in the spine that can be released and made available to us.

The student of Yoga knows that while adjustments, massages, steam, etc. may provide relief in certain disorders, it is only the methodical, *self-manipulation* of the back and spine, at least once each day, that truly strengthens the back and aids in separating the vertebrae. Many ailments have responded most favorably to the various stretching and strengthening techniques we will learn in this book. The Yogi also believes that a strong, elastic spine preserves the feeling and appearance of youthfulness; a classic Yogic axiom proclaims, "You are as young as your spine is flexible."

The Back Stretch posture and the Chest Expansion posture that follow will serve you in a number of ways. They will enable you to get the "feel" of the Yoga movements, of the slow motion, of the "holding" in the extreme positions, of the concentration of the mind on the various movements. Also, they will provide an excellent indication of how stiff and tense you may have become. The more inflexible you find yourself, the more urgent is your need, regardless of age, to work through this condition. Since Hatha Yoga is a *progressive* system of movement, your present degree of stiffness or weakness is inconsequential. If you will perform the exercises exactly as instructed, you will probably be astonished at how quickly your spine begins to regain its youthful elasticity. As this occurs not only do you experience a wonderful "spring" returning to your entire body, but you should notice that your mind reacts more quickly and with greater clarity. In cases of major back or spine disorders the student should receive the permission of his physician before undertaking the postures.

In this era of innumerable physical, emotional and mental disturbances it should be highly meaningful to learn that simple, methodical stretching can relieve tension and release energy!

Important

Establish firmly the need for graceful, slow motion movement. The extreme forward positions are held without movement. Counting must be rhythmic. The neck is completely relaxed in the forward bends. You are never to experience strain. Each day will enable you to bend farther forward.

Practice Information

Perform the calf pulls twice and the ankle pulls twice (or only the calf pulls four times).

FIG. 8—*Sit with your legs outstretched, feet touching.* In very slow motion *raise your arms and lean backward several inches (to tone the abdominal muscles). Head is back, look upward.*

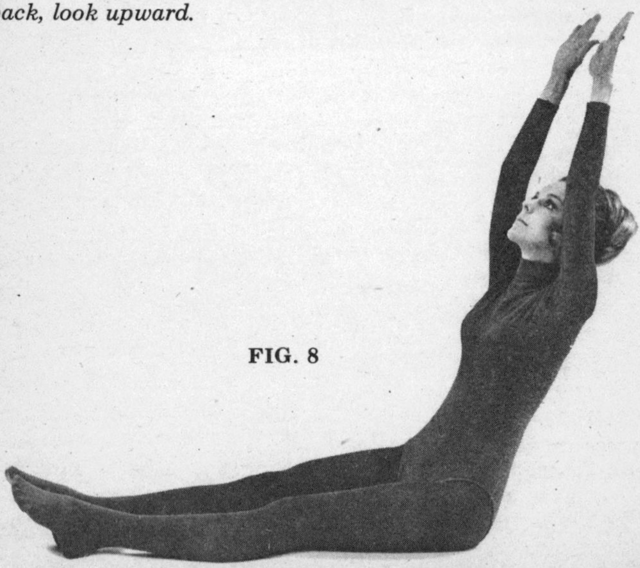

FIG. 8

FIG. 9

FIG. 10

FIG. 9 — In very slow motion, *with your arms outstretched, execute a forward "dive." Perform your movements with the grace, poise and balance of a ballet dancer.*

FIG. 10 — *Take a firm grip on your calves.*

FIG. 11

FIG. 11—*Pull against your calves and, in very slow motion, lower the trunk as far as it will go* without strain. *Elbows must bend outward; forehead is aimed at knees.*

Hold your extreme position, without motion *for a count of 10 (count rhythmically in approximate seconds).*

To reiterate: it is of no consequence how far down you are able to bring your trunk (only two inches would be satisfactory); what is essential is that you hold your extreme position without motion for a count of 10.

When the count of 10 is completed, in very slow motion, *straighten to an upright position and simultaneously raise your arms into the position of Fig. 8. Lean backward several inches. Repeat the slow motion "dive," once again hold the calves and gently pull the trunk down. Hold for 10 as before.*

FIG. 12

FIG. 12—*When the count of 10 is completed, repeat the movements of Figs. 8 and 9 but now attempt to reach farther down and hold your ankles. If this cannot be done* without strain, *revert to the calves.*

Pull against the ankles and lower the trunk as before. Hold for 10. Slowly straighten up and repeat the ankle movement.

When the count of 10 is completed, slowly straighten to the upright position. Rest your hands on your knees and relax for a few moments.

5 / CHEST EXPANSION
(Ardha Chakrasana)

OBJECTIVES OF THE CHEST EXPANSION: *Identical with those of the Back Stretch. In addition these movements firm the bust and develop the chest so that lung capacity may be increased. Also, an excellent exercise to remove the tired, cramped feeling from the shoulders.*

Important

Move in slow motion at all times. Keep in mind the image of the rhythmic poise and balance of a dancer. Do not bend farther backward or forward than depicted at present. Remember to hold your arms as high as possible throughout the exercise. Your neck is relaxed in both bending positions. Do not strain.

Practice Information

Perform the entire routine twice. Count 5 in the backward bend and 10 in the forward bend.

Many Yoga students perform the Chest Expansion several times during the day. Since it provides an immediate relief of tension for the back, spine and shoulders, it is an excellent exercise to practice after several hours of housework, sitting at a desk or driving. It requires no special exercise clothing; all you need is sufficient space. Some students take a "Yoga break" along with their "coffee break." They do the Chest Expansion, the Neck movements (that will be learned subsequently) and perform a few Complete Breaths seated at their desks. You cannot do your best work if your back, spine, shoulders or neck are tense and uncomfortable, or if your mind is tired. The Chest Expansion helps to combat all of these conditions. Try it and see.

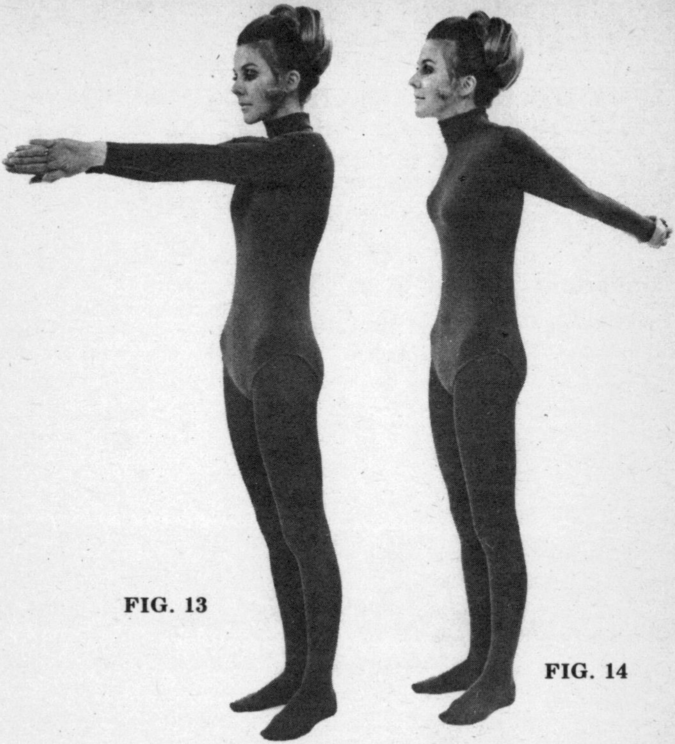

FIG. 13

FIG. 14

FIG. 13—*Stand with your heels together, arms at sides. In very slow, graceful motion bring your hands up so that they touch your chest.*

Slowly stretch the arms straight outward as far as possible (Fig. 13). Feel the elbows stretching.

FIG. 14—*Slowly bring the arms back. Hold them high, on a level with your shoulders.*

Now lower the arms slightly so that your fingers may be interlaced. When this has been done, raise the arms as high as possible without strain. Do not allow your trunk to bend forward.

FIG. 15

FIG. 16

FIG. 15—*Gently, without strain, bend backward slowly several inches. Do not go farther than illustrated. Look upward. Keep arms high (for stretching of the shoulders) and knees straight. Hold for a count of 5 without motion.*

FIG. 16—*Very slowly bend forward into the position illustrated. Do not go farther than depicted. Bring the arms over the back. Neck is limp and head is aimed toward knees. Hold without motion for 10.*

Slowly straighten to the upright position of Fig. 14. Pause for a moment and then repeat the backward and forward bends.

Straighten to an upright position, bring the arms down to the sides and relax.

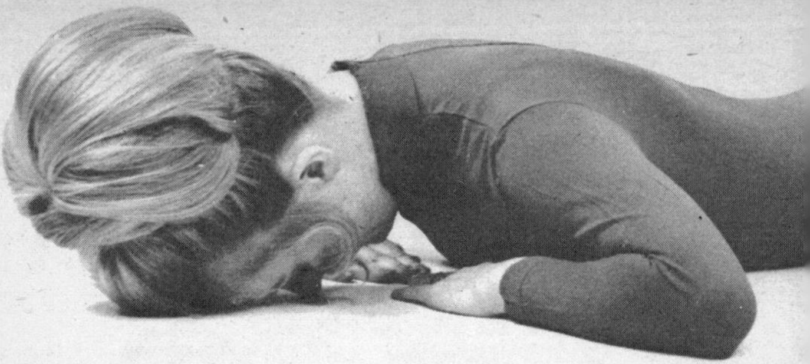

6 / COBRA *(Bhujangasana)*

OBJECTIVES OF THE COBRA:

Identical with those of the Back Stretch. Particular emphasis is placed on the entire spine and the lumbar area of the back.

Important

The greatest benefits are derived from the Cobra when the spine is continually curved inward while raising the trunk. You move so slowly that you can feel each vertebra, in turn, being manipulated. At no time does this exercise become a calisthenic "push-up" with a straight back. The Cobra imparts great elasticity to the spine which, once achieved, can easily be retained for life. If the position of Fig. 20 is too extreme for you, stop at Fig. 19; even Fig. 18 is satisfactory in the beginning. There is no rush. Your spine *wants* to stretch out and it will respond quickly to the Cobra movements.

Practice Information

Perform three times holding your extreme raised position for a count of 10.

Since deep relaxation is experienced following the Cobra, it is excellent for promoting a restful sleep. It has also proved helpful in cases of slipped discs (consult your physician).

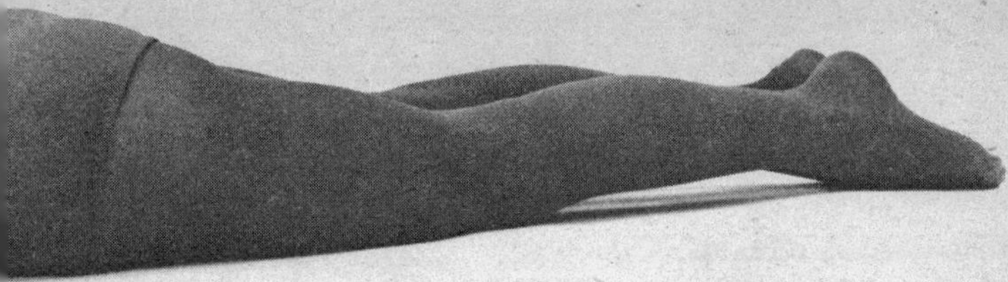

FIG. 17

FIG. 17—*Rest your forehead on the mat, arms at sides. relax the body; do not hold any muscles tense.*

Bring your hands up and place them beneath your shoulders as illustrated. Note the position of the hands; the fingers are together and pointing at right angles *to the shoulders.*

FIG. 18—*In very slow motion begin to raise your head and bend it backward.*

Push against the floor with your hands and begin to raise your trunk.

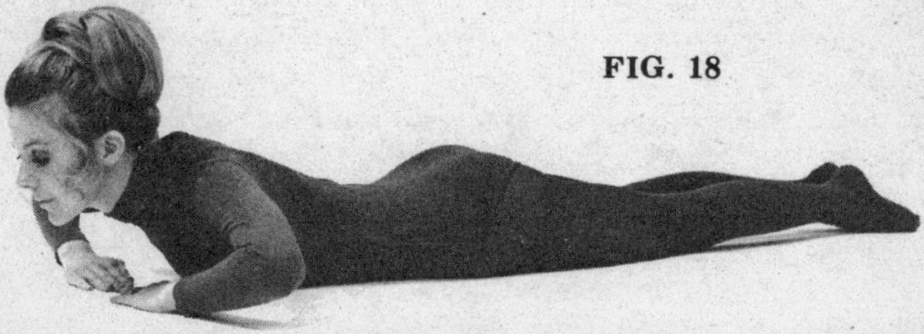

FIG. 18

FIG. 19

FIG. 20

FIG. 19—*In very slow motion continue to raise the trunk. The head bends backward and the spine is continually curved.*

FIG. 20—*The completed posture. Do not raise higher than depicted. Head is far back, eyes look upward. Elbows are still slightly bent. Spine is acutely arched. Legs are relaxed. Hold without motion for a count of 10.*

In very slow motion reverse the movements and lower your trunk until the forehead rests once again on the floor. Pause a few moments and repeat.

When you have completed the repetitions rest your cheek on the mat and allow your body to go completely limp.

7 / LOCUST *(Salabhasana)*

OBJECTIVES OF THE LOCUST:

To develop, strengthen and impart good muscle tone to the lower abdomen, groin, buttocks and arms.

Important

The raising of both legs in Fig. 22 is not easy. The important thing in the Locust, as in most of the more difficult Yoga postures, is the *attempt.* It is the repeated attempts that will gradually strengthen the muscles involved. Therefore, you must not be discouraged or neglect this excellent exercise. Remember, raising both legs only one inch will start you on your way. Each time you practice the Locust, the muscles of your abdomen and legs will grow that much stronger. Within a few weeks the position of Fig. 22 should be attained.

Practice Information

Raise the legs separately once; hold for 10.

Raise both legs three times; hold for 5.

Sports, calisthenics and our usual daily activities exercise certain muscles, but other vital ones, such as those involved in the Locust, are often neglected. The Locust is one of a number of firming and strengthening postures presented in this book that will enable you to maintain excellent muscle tone in every area of your body with a minimum expenditure of effort. Yoga does not seek to overdevelop muscles and to impart bulging biceps. Rather, it is concerned with the *resilience* of muscles so that the skin they support remains taut and does not become flabby or sag and the organs and glands they support (as, for example, in the abdominal area) maintain their correct position and do not "drop."

Those who are interested in natural development of the muscles to their full potential will find postures such as the Locust of great value.

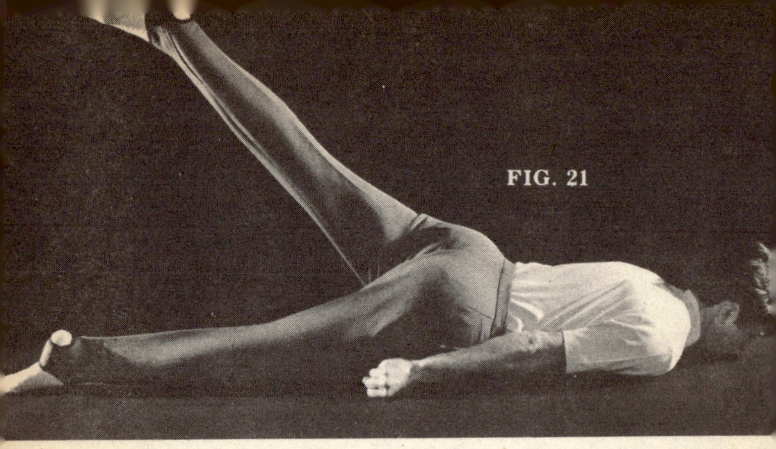
FIG. 21

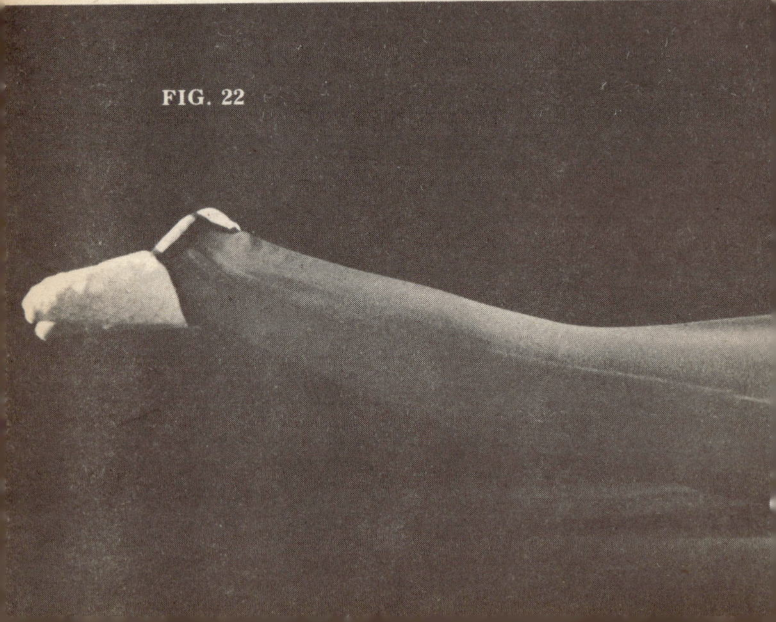
FIG. 22

FIG. 21—*Rest your chin on the mat. (Note,* chin *not fore-head as in the Cobra.)*

Make fists of your hands and place them thumbs down firmly on the floor at your sides.

Push against the floor with your fists and very slowly raise your left leg as high as possible. Knee is straight. Hold without motion for 10.

Very slowly lower left leg to the floor and raise the right. Hold for 10.

Very slowly lower right leg to the floor.

FIG. 22—*Inhale and* retain the breath.

Push hard against the floor and raise both legs a moderate distance. Only one inch is satisfactory in the beginning. Chin remains on mat, knees are straight, breath is held. Hold the raised position without motion for 5.

Very slowly *lower legs to the floor and simultaneously exhale. Relax a few moments. Inhale and repeat.*

Following the final repetition rest your cheek on the mat and relax completely.

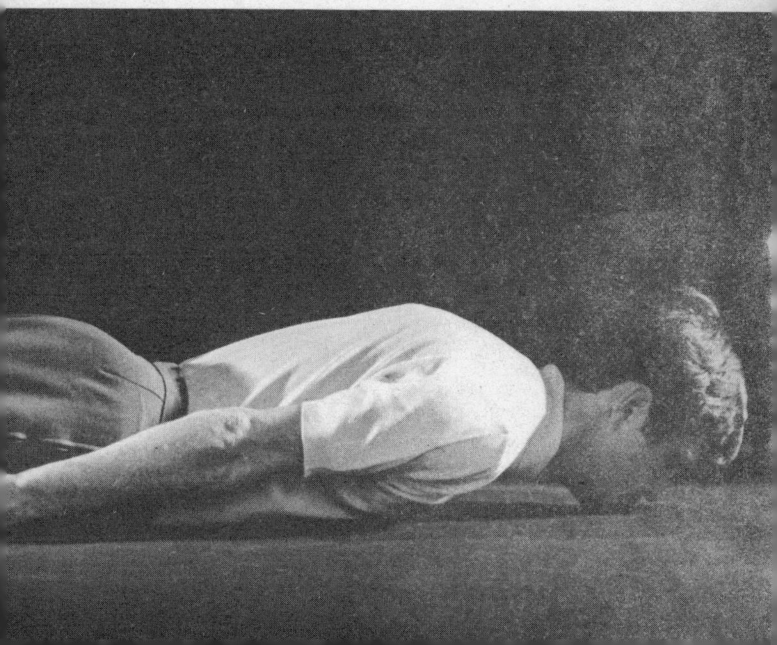

8 / BOW *(Dhanurasana)*

OBJECTIVES OF THE BOW:

To provide intensive strengthening for the back and spine; to develop the chest and bust; to improve posture.

Important

The Bow, like the Locust, is not easy; the repeated attempts will gradually bring success. The Bow is a powerful movement and must be executed slowly and cautiously. Do not jerk the trunk upward. Make certain to lower the knees and trunk in the directed order.

Practice Information

Perform three times; hold for 10.

If the position of Fig. 25 is too difficult, revert to Fig. 24, raise only the trunk three times and hold for 10.

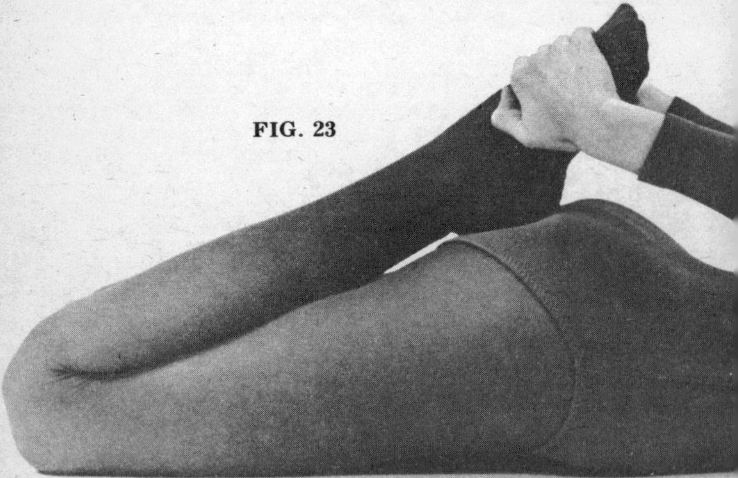

FIG. 23

FIG. 23—*Rest your chin on the mat, as in the Locust. Bend knees, bring feet toward back. Reach behind you and attempt to hold feet as illustrated. Chin remains on floor.*

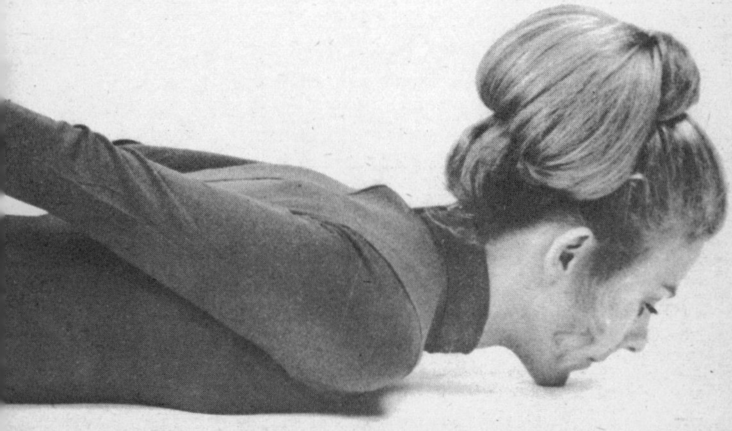

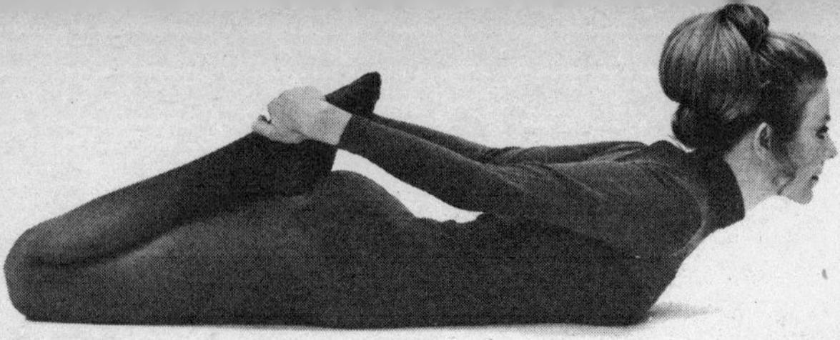

FIG. 24

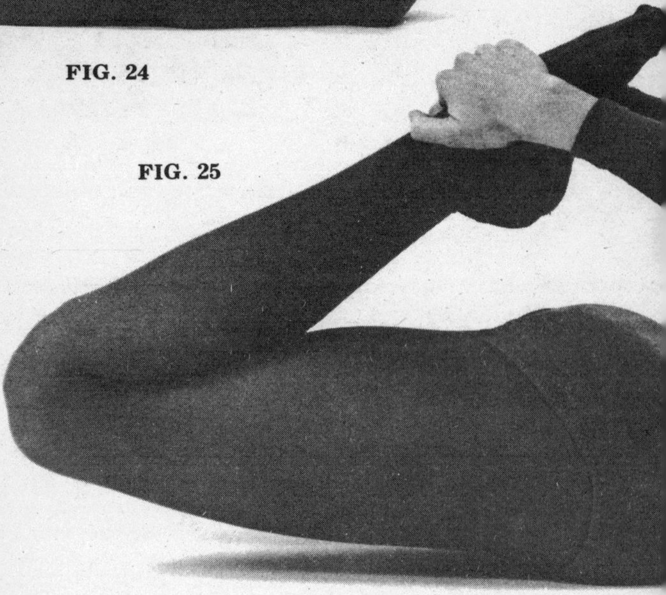

FIG. 25

FIG. 24—*Slowly and cautiously raise only your head.*

FIG. 25—*Pull hard against feet; raise trunk and knees a short distance from the floor. Head is back, knees as close together as possible. Breathe normally. Hold without motion for 10.*

Lower knees to floor, retain hold on feet. Lower chin to floor, retain hold on feet. Pause for a few moments and repeat.

Following the final repetition lower knees and chin to floor and then slowly return the feet to the floor. Rest cheek on the mat and relax completely.

9 / SIDE BEND *(Nitambasana)*

OBJECTIVES OF THE SIDE BEND:

To improve the contour of the figure and help remove excess inches as necessary.

Practice Information

Perform the short bends once to each side. Hold for 10.
Perform the intermediate bends once to each side.
Hold for 10.

FIG. 26

FIG. 26 — *Stand with the heels together.*

Gracefully raise arms overhead. Palms face each other.

Very slowly bend your trunk and head a short distance to the left. Do not go farther than illustrated. Arms remain parallel. Hold without motion for 10.

Slowly straighten to the upright position.

Now bend, in an identical manner, a short distance to the right. Hold for 10.

Slowly straighten to the upright position.

FIG. 27 — *Once again bend slowly to the left and increase the distance several inches as illustrated. Make certain that the arms remain parallel. Hold for 10.*

Slowly straighten to the upright position.

FIG. 27

FIG. 28—*Bend the identical distance to the right. Hold for 10.*

Straighten to the upright position.

Slowly lower arms to the sides and relax.

10 /TRIANGLE *(Trikonasana)*

OBJECTIVES OF THE TRIANGLE:

To firm the sides and thighs; to reduce excess weight in the waistline.

Important

In Figs. 31 and 32 make certain your arm is brought far over your head into the position illustrated. This is essential to experience the maximum firming of the sides.

Practice Information

Perform twice on each side, alternating left-right. Hold each bend for 10.

The Side Bend and Triangle postures are excellent for streamlining the figure with minimum effort. The Yoga exercises are proof that it is not the *amount* of activity (many repetitions of bends, push-ups, rolls, etc.) that acts to regulate and control weight. It is the *type* of movement *(where* the emphasis is placed and how long it is *held)* that is the essential factor.

FIG. 29—*Assume a stance with your legs approximately two feet apart.*

Gracefully raise your arms to shoulder level.

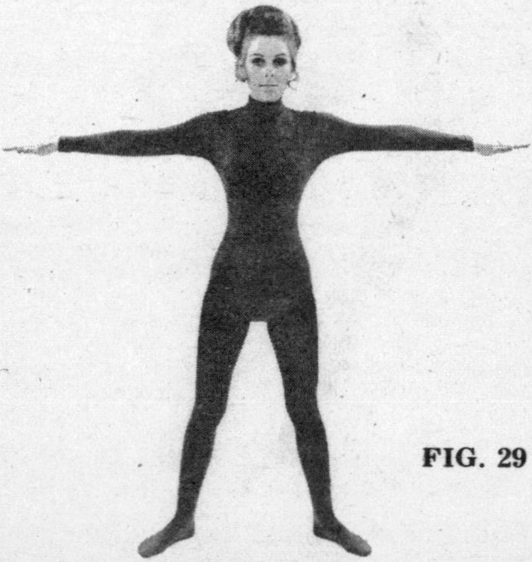

FIG. 29

FIG. 30

FIG. 31

FIG. 32

FIG. 30—*Slowly bend to the left and take a firm hold on your left calf. Note that right arm is brought over the head.*

FIG. 31—*Pull on the calf and lower the trunk as illustrated. The left elbow bends and the right arm is now brought over the head so that it is parallel with the floor. Knees remain straight. Neck is relaxed. Hold for 10.*

Slowly straighten to the upright position of Fig. 29.

FIG. 32—*Perform the identical movements to the right. Hold for 10.*

Slowly straighten to the upright position. Repeat the movements once on each side. After the final repetition, lower the arms gracefully to the sides, draw the legs together and relax.

11 / BACKWARD BEND
(Supta-Vajrasana)

OBJECTIVES OF THE BACKWARD BEND:
To strengthen and impart flexibility to the feet and ankles.

Important

Remain seated on heels throughout exercise. Note carefully the correct position of hands and fingers. Knees are held together.

Practice Information

Perform once in the moderate position of Fig. 35. Hold for 10.

Perform once in the extreme position of Fig. 36. Hold for 10.

This posture places stress on the feet and ankles. If you have neglected these areas in your previous exercising, you may find them weak and inflexible. If this is the case you should proceed cautiously in this exercise and place only as much weight on the heels as is comfortable. Simply sitting in the position of Fig. 33 for a count of 10 will gradually enable you to accomplish the more extreme positions. The greater the stiffness you experience, the more urgent it is to practice the Backward Bend, patiently and cautiously.

FIG. 33—*Sit on your heels. Knees are together.*

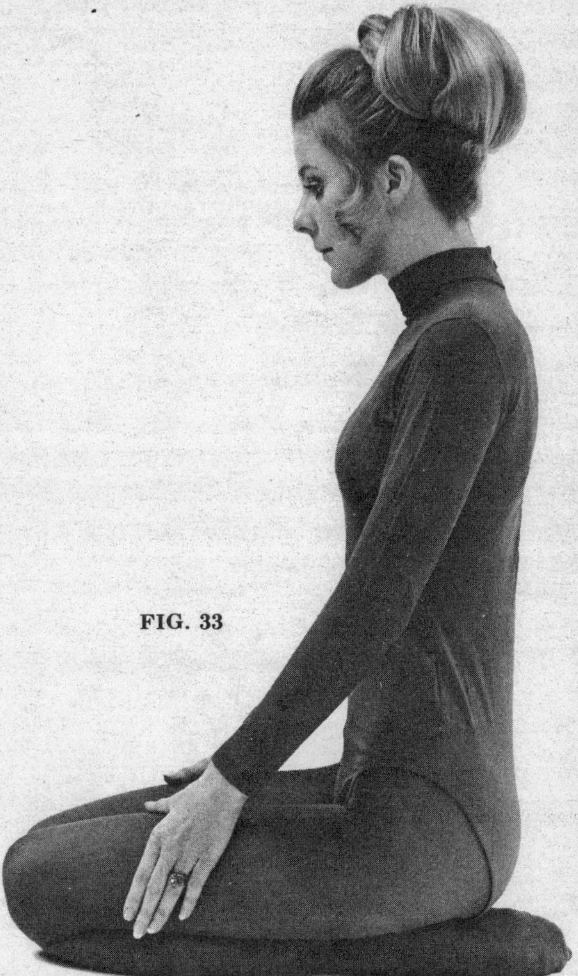

FIG. 33

FIG. 34

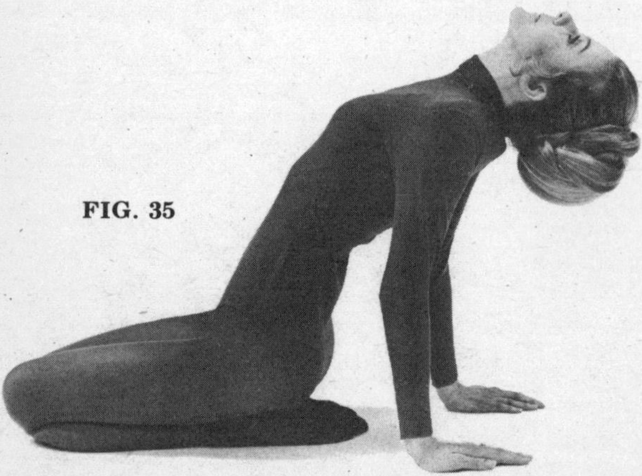

FIG. 35

FIG. 36

FIG. 34—*Place your hands on the floor and cautiously inch backward a moderate distance. Note position of the fingers: they point behind you.*

FIG. 35—*Remain seated on your heels with your knees together. Slowly arch your trunk upward and lower your head backward. Hold for 10.*

FIG. 36—*Raise head. Cautiously move hands as far backward as possible without strain. Fingers point behind you and knees remain together. Now raise trunk as high as possible with spine arched and lower head backward. Hold for 10.*

Raise head and lower trunk. Slowly move hands and trunk forward to position of Fig. 33. Relax.

12 / SHOULDER STAND *(Sarvangasana)*

OBJECTIVES OF THE SHOULDER STAND:

To help promote good blood circulation; to stimulate the thyroid gland as an aid in weight regulation; to relax the legs; to bring an increased supply of blood into the upper regions of the organism.

Since most of our daily activities are performed in sitting and standing positions, it is of extreme value to periodically invert the body so that the blood circulation may, in a sense, be "reversed." There are a number of exercises in this study that invert the body in various degrees; the two most extreme postures are the Head Stand and the Shoulder Stand.

The benefits of the Shoulder Stand, regardless of your age, are many and important. Gravity is always at work, exerting its pull on various organs and glands. With the body in the inverted position they are temporarily relieved of the usual gravitational pressure and are permitted to "relax." This is also true of the veins, and arteries, and people suffering with varicose veins in their legs and hardening of the arteries have experienced improvement in these conditions through the Shoulder Stand posture.

Further, the heart must continually pump against gravity to bring the blood into those areas situated above it. Again, in the Shoulder Stand it is obvious that this operation is greatly facilitated. Of extreme interest is the effect of the inverted position on the thyroid gland. Situated in the neck the thyroid plays a vital role in weight regulation and control. The blood stimulates and brings nourishment to the thyroid so that if the circulation is inadequate the thyroid may not function properly. You will note that the extreme positions of the Shoulder Stand cause the blood to flow directly into the neck, and the resultant effect on the thyroid has been, for numerous students, most pronounced with regard to weight regulation.

In most systems of exercising the blood is made to circulate more quickly, often much too quickly, by means of greatly increased activity (calisthenics, jogging, etc.). The completed Shoulder Stand posture is an outstanding Yogic example of improving blood circulation without any movement whatsoever!

Important

Any angle of inversion is better than none. Therefore, if the position of Fig. 39 is too extreme at this time, remain in that of Fig. 38. If you cannot raise your hips from the floor, simply raise your legs and hold them upright for one minute. In some cases, swinging the legs back over the head with strong momentum will enable the hips to be raised.

Practice Information

Perform the Shoulder Stand once, holding the extreme position for one minute in the beginning and gradually working up to three minutes. Advanced students often hold this position for up to ten minutes because of its relaxing and refreshing properties. You should be able to glance at a watch or clock since the progressive timing is important.

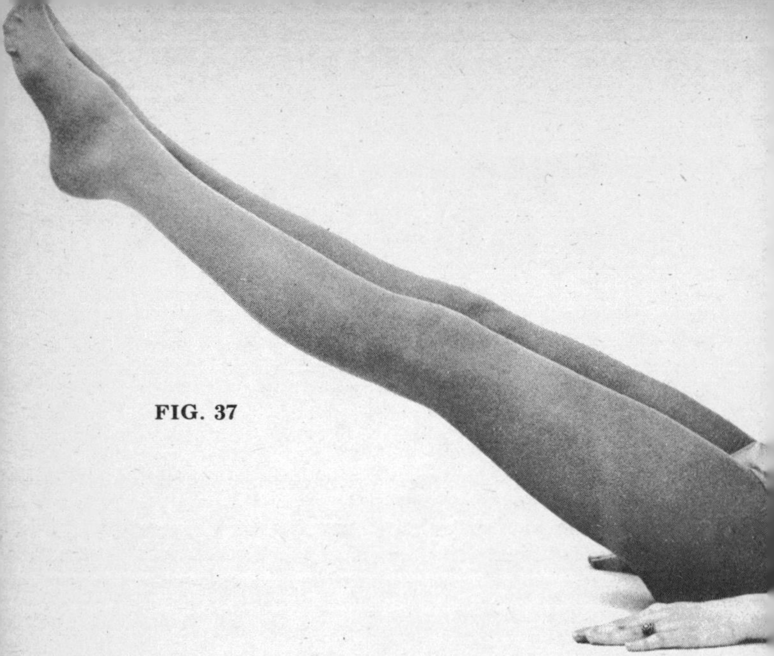

FIG. 37

FIG. 37—*Rest in the Deep Relaxation Posture for several moments.*

Place your palms against the floor; tense your abdominal and leg muscles.

Push palms against floor and slowly raise your legs; knees are straight.

FIG. 38—*Swing your legs back over your head. As soon as your hips leave the floor, brace your hands against them to support lower back.*

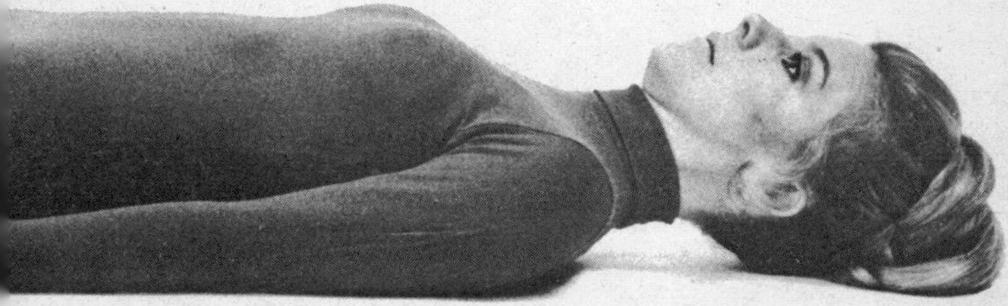

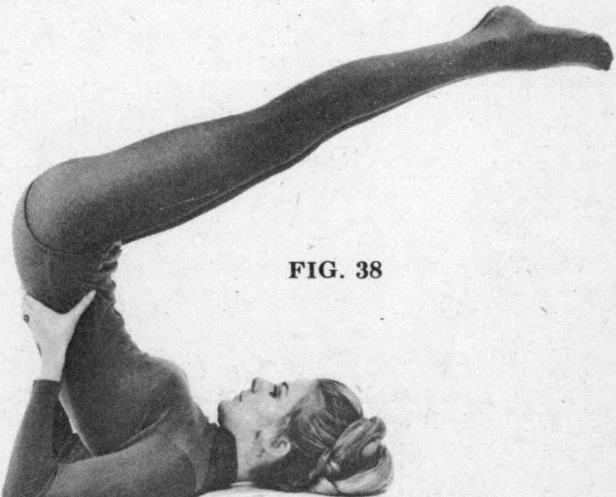

FIG. 38

FIG. 39

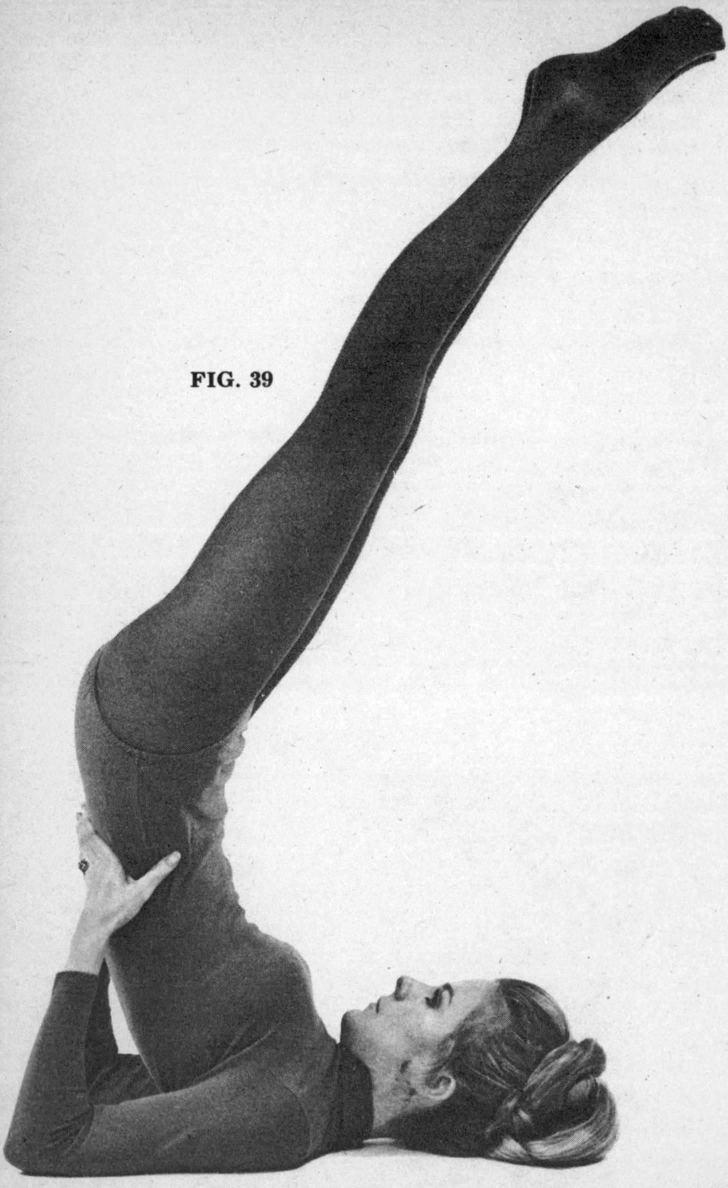

FIG. 39—*Very slowly and cautiously straighten to a moderate upright position, approximately as illustrated. It is suggested that you do not straighten farther than this position at present. Legs are relaxed; eyes may be closed. Hold as indicated under "Practice Information."*

It is essential to return the legs to the floor exactly as directed.

Bend your knees and lower them to your forehead.

Place palms back on the floor.

Arch your neck upward (to keep back of head on floor) and gracefully roll forward.

When your hips touch the floor straighten your legs into the position of Fig. 37.

Slowly lower legs to the floor and relax completely for one minute.

---

13 / SIDE RAISE
(Uttitha Merudandasana)

OBJECTIVES OF THE SIDE RAISE:
To firm and strengthen the abdomen, legs and buttocks.

Important

In Fig. 42 your legs must remain together and be raised straight up from the floor. They must not move behind or in front of your trunk.

Practice Information

Raise one leg once and both legs three times. Hold each raise for 10. Perform first on left side, then on right.

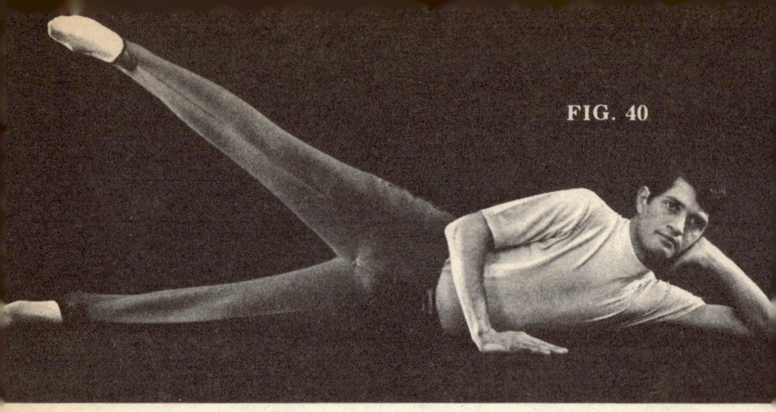

FIG. 40

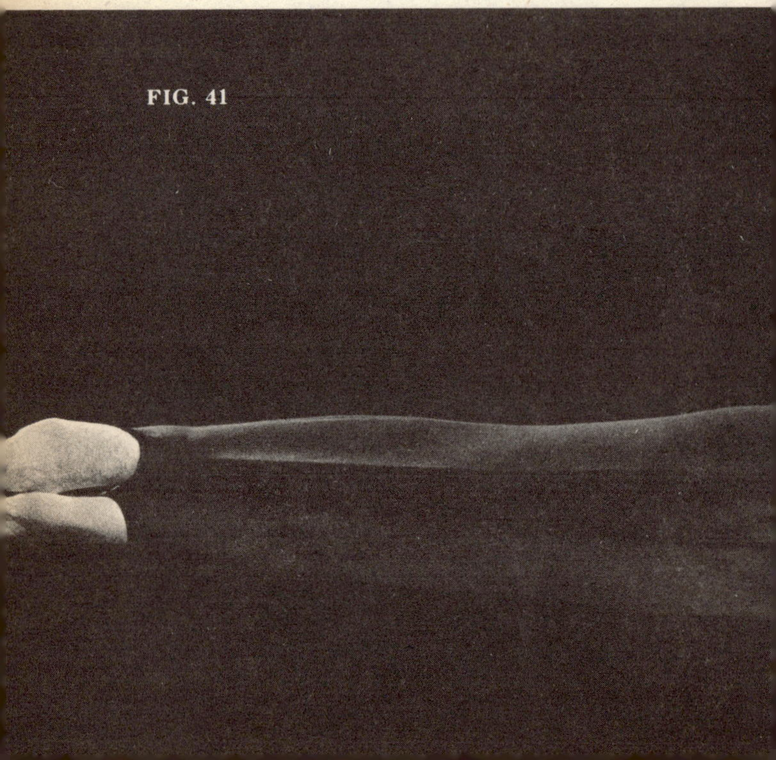

FIG. 41

FIG. 40—*Lie on your left side with legs together and left cheek resting in left palm. Left elbow is as illustrated. Place right hand firmly on floor.*

Push against floor with right hand and slowly raise right leg as high as possible. Hold for 10.

Slowly lower right leg.

FIG. 41—*Push against floor with right hand and slowly raise both legs a moderate distance from the floor. Do not raise higher than illustrated. Legs must remain together and be raised in a line with your trunk. Hold for 10.*

Slowly lower the legs to the floor. Relax a moment and repeat.

Following the final repetition, roll onto right side. Perform the identical movements, raising the left leg once and then both legs.

14 / BACK PUSH-UP *(Kamdharasana)*

OBJECTIVES OF THE BACK PUSH-UP:

To firm and strengthen the abdomen, legs, buttocks and arms.

Important

Knees are held together. Do not raise higher than illustrated.

Practice Information

Perform five times. Hold each raise for 10.

FIG. 42—*Lie on your back. Bend knees and bring feet in as far as possible. Place hands as illustrated. Note that fingers are together, pointing behind you.*

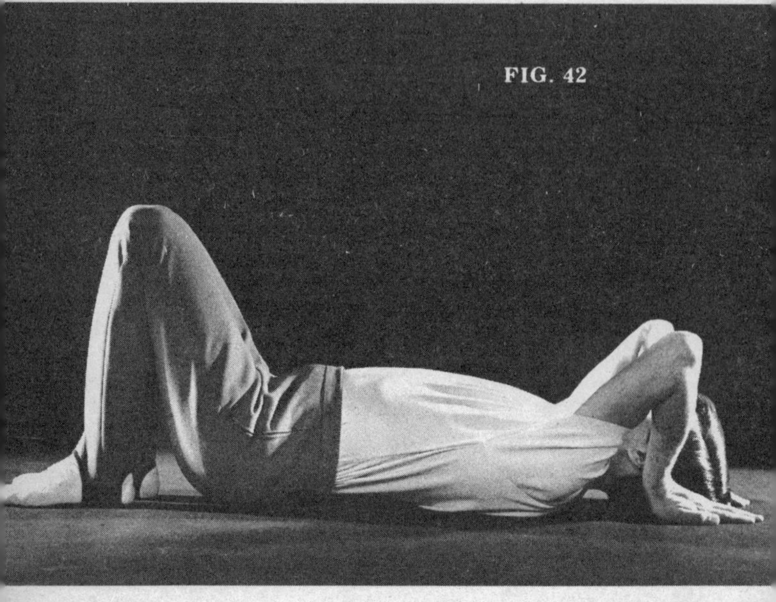

FIG. 42

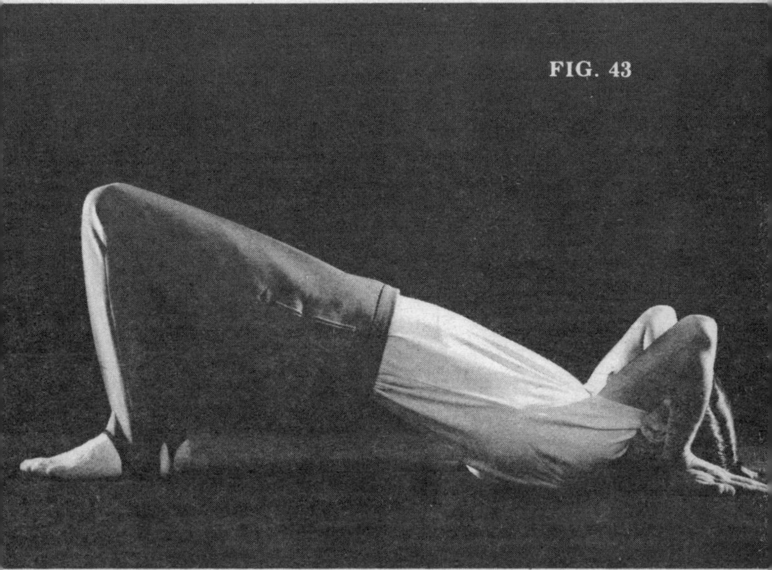

FIG. 43

FIG. 43—*Push hands and feet against floor and slowly raise trunk to position illustrated. Knees are together. Hold for 10.*

Slowly lower trunk to floor. Relax a moment and repeat.

15 / KNEE and THIGH STRETCH
(Bhadrasana)

OBJECTIVES OF THE KNEE and THIGH STRETCH:

To promote flexibility in the knees; to stretch and firm the thighs.

Important

In initial attempts you may be able to lower your knees only a few inches. Simply hold whatever extreme position you can attain for the count of 10. The stiff, tight ligaments and muscles involved will gradually "give." Make certain that the trunk is erect throughout the movements.

Practice Information

Perform three times. Hold each stretch for 10.

This is one of the stretching postures that can be performed when it is desirable to remove tension and revitalize the legs.

FIG. 44—*In a seated posture place clasped hands around feet. Bring heels in as far as possible. Spine is held straight.*

FIG. 45—*Pull up against feet and lower knees toward floor. Keep spine erect. Hold for 10.*

Allow the knees to return to the position of Fig. 45. Repeat.

FIG. 44

FIG. 45

16 / TWIST *(Ardha Matsyendrasana)*

OBJECTIVES OF THE TWIST:

To provide a quick relief for stiffness and tension in the spine; to promote flexibility.

Important

Study the illustrations to make certain that your arms and legs assume the correct positions and that you are twisting in the correct direction. The way in which the spine is manipulated sometimes causes confusion in the beginning. It is important that the head turn as far as possible, almost resting on the shoulder, to aid the spine in twisting.

Practice Information

Perform two twists to the left and two to the right. Hold each for 10.

These twisting movements usually provide an immediate loosening for the entire spine. We have previously manipulated the spine outward (as in the Back Stretch) and inward (as in the Cobra). Here we add another vital movement by manipulating the spine in a "corkscrew" fashion. The vertebrae respond well to this twisting, which is why it is a standard technique of the chiropractor. The position of Fig. 47 partially "locks" the lower back and spine and, against this lock, the middle and upper regions are turned.

A more intensive twist is introduced in the Intermediate section.

FIG. 46 — *Sit with your legs outstretched.*

Cross your left leg over your right as illustrated.

Place your left hand firmly on the floor behind your back.

FIG. 47 — *Cross your* right arm over your left knee *and take a firm hold on your right knee.*

FIG. 46

FIG. 47

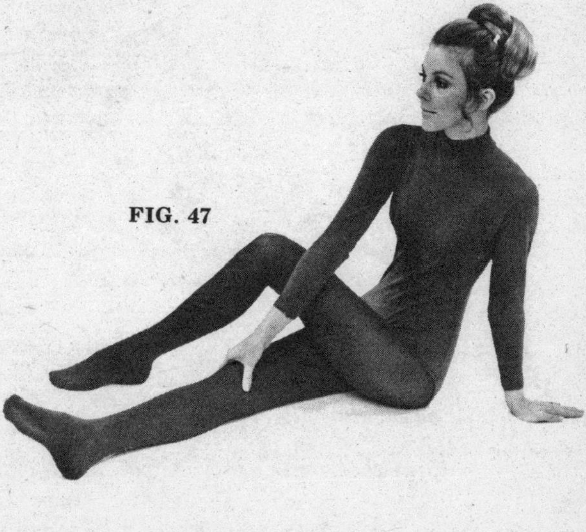

FIG. 48

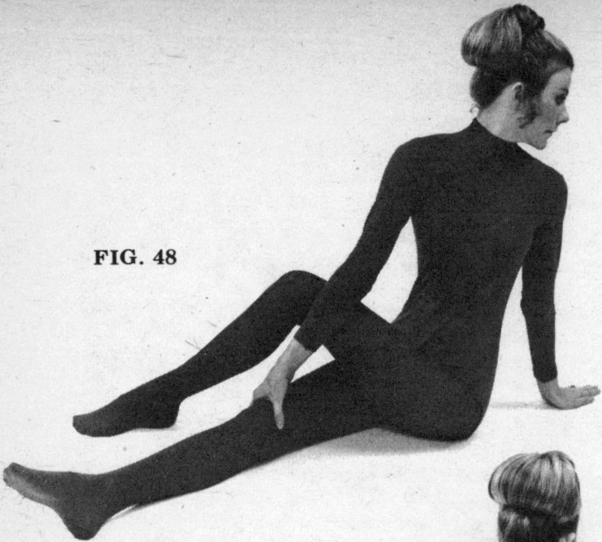

FIG. 49

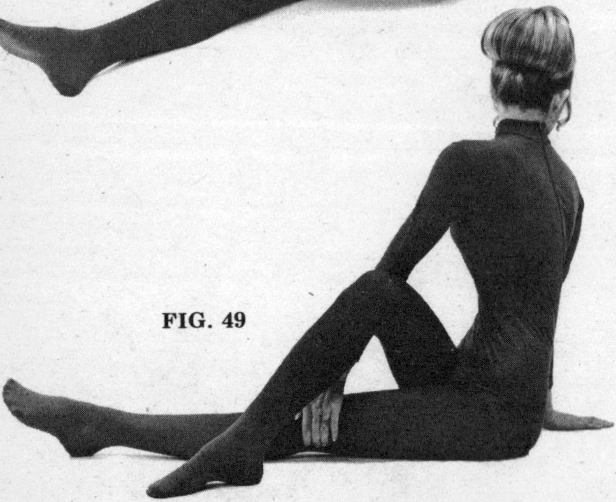

FIG. 48—*Very slowly twist your trunk and head as far to the* left *as possible. Hold without motion for 10.*

Return to the position of Fig. 47. Repeat.

FIG. 49—*Perform the identical movements on the* right *side.*

Following the final repetition, turn frontward, stretch your legs straight out and relax.

17 / LEG CLASP *(Padahastasana)*

OBJECTIVES OF THE LEG CLASP:

To provide an intensive stretch for the entire leg; to promote flexibility throughout the spine.

Important

Note that it is the *back* of the hands that are braced against the knees. Knees must not bend.

Practice Information

Perform twice. Hold each stretch for 10.

FIG. 50—*In a standing position bend slowly forward and clasp your hands behind your knees.*

FIG. 50

FIG. 51

FIG. 51—*Pull against the knees and draw trunk down as far as possible. Eventually forehead will touch the knees as depicted. Hold your extreme position without motion for 10.*

Relax the trunk and slowly raise it to the position of Fig. 50. Keep the hands clasped.

Repeat.

Unclasp hands and very slowly raise your trunk to the upright position.

18 / RISHI'S POSTURE

OBJECTIVE OF THE RISHI'S POSTURE:

To aid in equalizing the sides. (One side is frequently weaker, shorter or less developed than the other.)

Important

Move with the grace and poise of a dancer. In Fig. 56 make every attempt to see the back of the hand. If this is not possible, move the hand to hold the knee rather than the calf; this will make the twist easier. Knees must remain straight.

Practice Information

Perform three times to each side; alternate left-right. Hold each bend for 10.

FIG. 52—*In a standing position, with heels together, slowly raise arms so that hands meet in front at eye level.*

FIG. 52

FIG. 53—*Fix your gaze on the back of the hands and very slowly turn trunk to the left.*

FIG. 54—*Continue the twist until the 90 degree position is reached.*

FIG. 54

FIG. 55—*Study the illustration. The right hand moves slowly down the right leg and holds the right calf firmly. The left arm moves behind you and the gaze follows the left hand.*

FIG. 56—*The completed posture. The left arm has moved to the overhead position and the gaze is on the back of the left hand. Hold without motion for 10.*

Slowly raise your trunk to the upright position and bring arms into the position of Fig. 52.

Now twist to the right *and perform the identical movements exchanging the words "right" and "left" in the above directions.*

Slowly straighten upright to the position of Fig. 52. Lower arms to sides and relax.

FIG. 56

19 / DANCER'S POSTURE *(Urvasana)*

OBJECTIVES OF THE DANCER'S POSTURE:

To promote balance, grace and poise; to firm and strengthen the legs.

Important

Very slow motion is essential in this exercise. Knees should point straight ahead and remain close together in the lowering and raising movements. If you lose your balance, pause a moment and begin again. If you continue to lose your balance, attempt the movements three times, then go on to the next exercise. Within several days of practice your balance will greatly improve. Note that in Fig. 58 *there is no pause.* You begin immediately to push up; this affords maximum strengthening for the legs. Raise high on your toes to strengthen feet and ankles. If your balance is lost at any point, simply begin again. Repetition will result in complete success.

Practice Information

Perform five times. There is no pause in the lowered position. The toes position is held for 5.

FIG. 57—*In a standing position with heels together rest your hands on your head as illustrated. Palms are pressed together.*

FIG. 58—In very slow motion *lower the body until buttocks touch heels. Knees remain close together.*

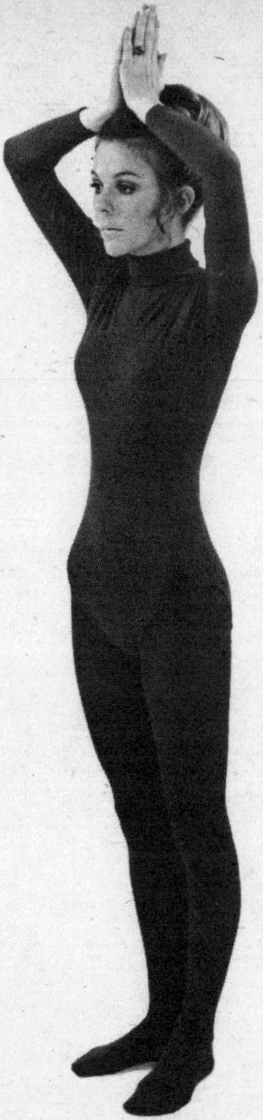

FIG. 57

FIG. 58

FIG. 59

FIG. 59 — Without pause *raise slowly to the upright position and come up high on toes. Hold for 5 as steady as possible.*

Lower soles of feet to floor. Repeat.

Following final repetition lower arms gracefully to sides and relax.

20 / BALANCE POSTURE
(Natarajasana)

OBJECTIVES OF THE BALANCE POSTURE:
To gain control of the balance; to impart equilibrium and poise.

The practice of Yoga imparts to the student an acute awareness of the beauty and power inherent in the body. He gradually senses that there is a spiritual aspect of the organism that previously may not have been perceived and the truth of the statement, "The body is the temple of the spirit" becomes a personal experience. The distinctions among what are usually conceived of as "body," "mind" and "spirit" gradually diminish and there occurs a merger or unification of the seemingly diverse aspects of our being. The realization that one can indeed function as an *integrated whole* is extremely meaningful; it effects a profound positive change in every aspect of life and paves the way for achieving the more advanced objectives of Yoga. (See my book on *Meditation.*)

The physical techniques that we are studying in this book were originally designed to achieve just such an integration of body, mind and spirit. If the student understands that there is much more involved in this practice than physical fitness or improving the figure, he will execute all of the movements in a very serious manner and with great attentiveness. The importance of this will be emphasized in our Intermediate Section.

In its attempt to achieve harmony and integration Hatha Yoga stresses the need for *coordination* of one's physical movements. We wish to develop a strong sense of balance and the ability to move, at all times, with grace and poise. The two previous exercises, Rishi's and Dancer's Postures, are partially for this purpose; the posture we are about to learn is designed solely to gain complete control of the balance. When these various "balance" postures are mastered, the body will assume an inescapable appearance of beauty and poise amidst all of its activities.

Important

Arm must move backward; head must also drop slightly backward. As with the Dancer's Posture, if you lose your balance at any point in the exercise, pause a moment and then begin again. If you are unsuccessful in three attempts proceed to next exercise. *Never laugh at yourself when balance is lost.* Maintain a serious attitude.

Practice Information

Perform three times with right arm raised; three times with left arm raised. Hold each stretch for 5.

FIG. 60 — *In a standing position with heels together slowly and gracefully raise your right arm overhead.*

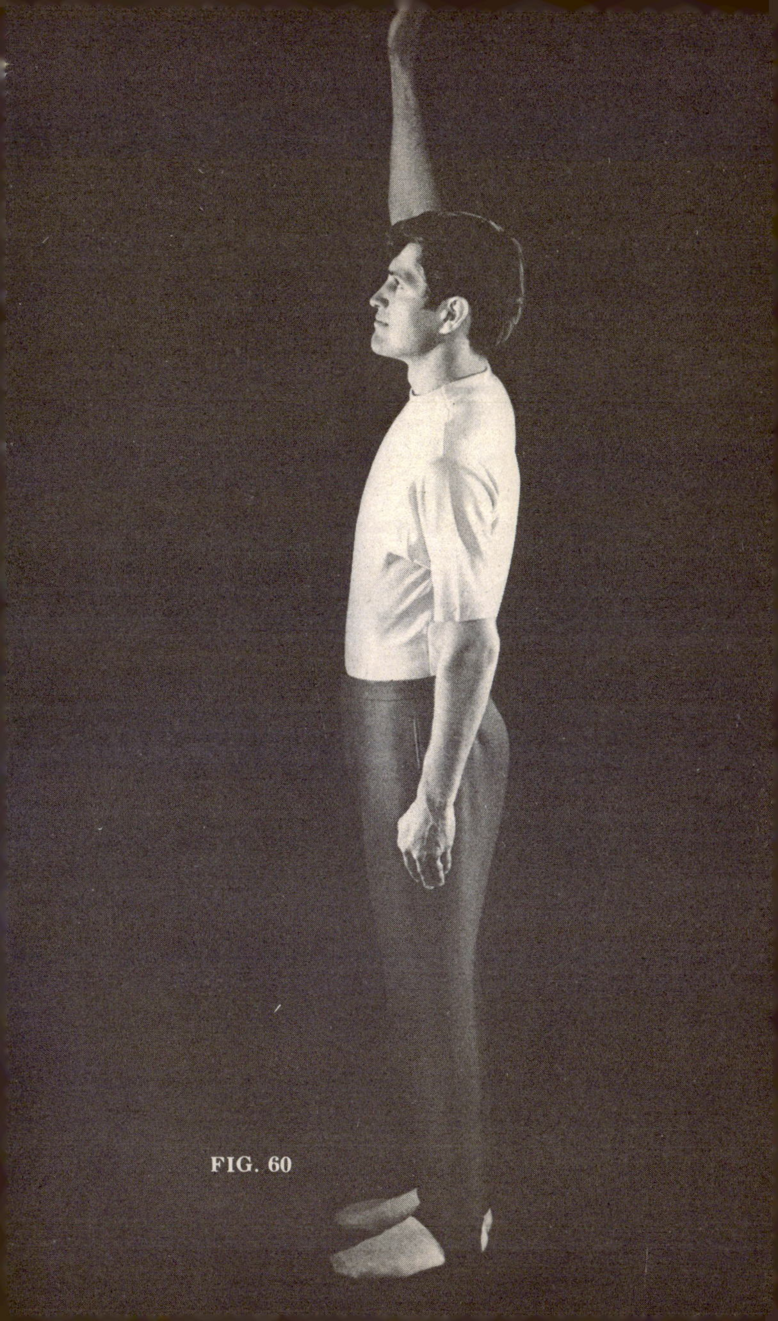

FIG. 60

FIG. 61

FIG. 61—*Shift the weight onto the right leg. Bend your left knee and raise your left foot so that your left hand can hold it.*

FIG. 62—*Pull up on left foot. Simultaneously look upward; drop head slightly backward and move upraised arm backward a few inches as illustrated. Hold as steady as possible for 5.*

Slowly return to the position of Fig. 60. Repeat.

Perform identical movements with left arm raised. Exchange the words "right" and "left" in the above directions.

Following the final repetition lower arm and leg and relax.

FIG. 62

21 / ABDOMINAL EXERCISE
(Uddiyana)

OBJECTIVES OF THE ABDOMINAL EXERCISE:

To tone the abdominal muscles; to reduce excess abdominal weight; to stimulate various organs of the viscera.

We have previously stated the necessity of approaching the health and care of the organism from a *total* standpoint. As such, we practice Yoga exercises designed not only for the muscles or for good circulation, but for the various systems of the body, the nervous, endocrine, respiratory, etc. Even the digestive system is taken into account. In the abdominal movements we are about to learn, the Yogic concept of "internal exercising" becomes evident. The following five pages are concerned with gaining control of the abdominal muscles through *contractions.* The Intermediate Section presents the technique for *lifting* the entire abdominal area. These movements provide stimulation for the intestines, colon and the peristaltic action; as such, they become invaluable and are utilized by Yoga students throughout their lives.

The problem of constipation has often been entirely overcome through the Abdominal Exercise. I have advised students to drink four to six ounces of cool water with a pinch of lemon upon arising (the stomach must be empty), wait for two or three minutes and then perform the Abdominal Exercise as directed. Once the immediate problem has been solved, a Yogic diet (or a modified variation of it) and periodic practice of the abdominal movements should prevent its recurrence. As a by-product of these movements excess pounds and inches are often lost and the abdomen becomes firm. It is important to remember that the tone of the abdominal wall must be maintained to prevent its prolapse and the subsequent weakening of the organs and glands that it supports.

This exercise will prove of special value to all those whose work requires them to remain in a seated position for several hours each day. Invest whatever time and effort is necessary to thoroughly master the technique.

Important

The degree of your contraction is unimportant in the beginning. If you can move your abdomen only one inch in both directions, you will improve with each day's practice. In Fig. 65, don't simply "relax" the abdomen or "push" it out. Attempt a sudden, forceful "snapping" movement with the abdominal muscles. Make certain your starting position is correct in Figs. 66 and 67.

Practice Information

Perform ten times in seated position.
Perform five times in standing position.
Perform five times in all-fours position.
Hold each contraction for 5.

The three postures place the abdomen and the visceral organs and glands in various positions. The seated contractions are good for reducing excess pounds and inches; the standing movements can be utilized for aiding the elimination process; the all-fours position is excellent for a "dropped" (prolapsed) abdomen and for after-birth exercising. All positions will firm and tone the abdominal muscles.

FIG. 63—*Sit in a cross-legged posture. Rest hands on knees. Pull your abdomen in by contracting the muscles as much as possible. Hold for 5.*

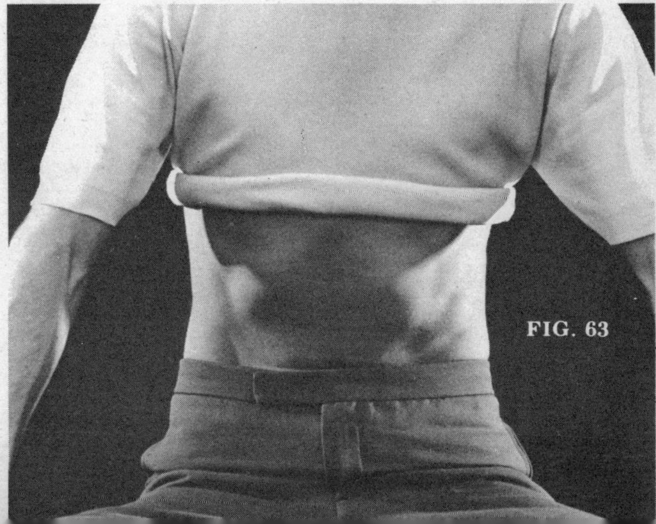

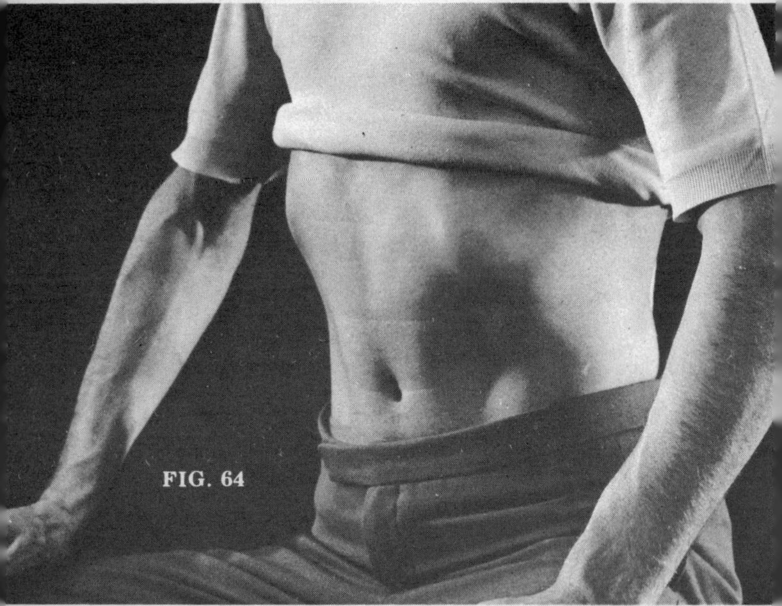

FIG. 64

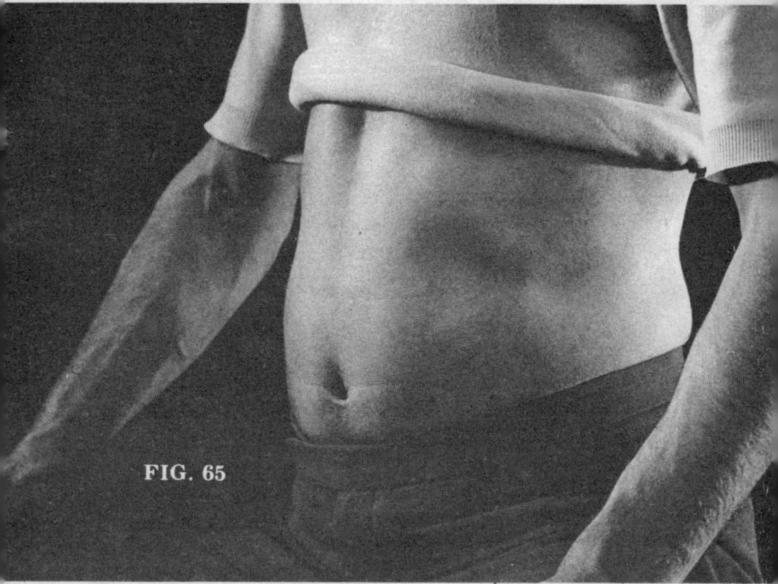

FIG. 65

FIG. 64—*A closeup of the contraction.*

FIG. 65—*Upon completion of the count of 5 attempt to "snap" the abdomen as far out as possible.*

Without pause *repeat the contraction and hold for 5. Perform 10 times. Relax. Stand up slowly.*

FIG. 66

FIG. 67

FIG. 66—*Execute the identical movements in this standing position. Study the illustration. Knees bend slightly outward. Hands are placed firmly on your thighs with all fingers, including thumb, pointing inward.*

Perform 5 times. With each contraction push down hard on the thighs. Hold each contraction for 5. Snap the abdomen out.

Following the last repetition slowly straighten upright and relax.

FIG. 67—*This is the All-Fours position. Study illustration. Legs are together, palms firmly on floor, arms parallel with knees, head lowered.*

Perform 5 times.

Following final repetition return to the cross-legged posture and relax.

22 / ALTERNATE LEG STRETCH
(Janusirasana)

OBJECTIVES OF THE ALTERNATE LEG STRETCH:

To firm, strengthen, revitalize and remove all tension from the legs.

Important

Remember that no strain is to be experienced. If the ankle position is too difficult, revert to the calf. Elbows must bend outward in the pulling movements. Back of knee must remain on floor. Neck is completely relaxed in forward bends. You may notice the movements are easier with one leg than the other. This is of no consequence at present. Gradually the sides should become even.

Practice Information

With the left leg outstretched, perform twice in the calf and once in the ankle positions. (Or, if necessary, three times in the calf position.) Hold each stretch for 10. Perform the identical movements with the right leg outstretched.

FIG. 68

FIG. 69

FIG. 68—*Sit with your legs outstretched.*

Take hold of your right foot and place the right heel as illustrated. The sole rests against (not under) the left thigh.

FIG. 69—*In very slow motion raise your arms overhead and lean backward several inches. Head is back, look upward.*

FIG. 70

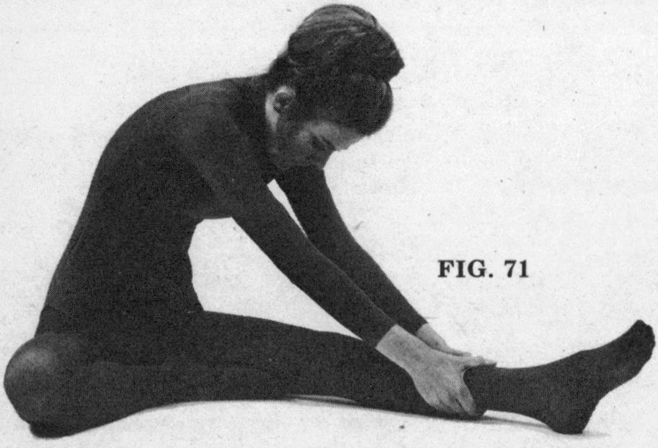

FIG. 71

FIG. 72

FIG. 70—*In very slow motion, with your arms outstretched, execute a forward "dive."*

FIG. 71—*Take a firm grip on your left calf. Do not be concerned if your right knee is raised from the floor.*

FIG. 72—*Pull against your calf and, in very slow motion, lower your trunk as far as possible without strain. Elbows bend outward, forehead is aimed at knee. Hold for 10.*

Slowly straighten upright and return to the position of Fig. 69.

Repeat the stretch and hold for 10.

Slowly straighten upright and return to the position of Fig. 69.

FIG. 73

FIG. 73—*Execute the slow motion forward dive and this time attempt to hold the ankle. (If this is not possible, revert to the calf.)*

Pull against the ankle and lower your trunk as previously. The stretching of the leg is now more intensive. Hold for 10.

Slowly straighten upright. Straighten right leg. Rest hands on knees and relax.

Perform the identical movements with the right *leg outstretched. Exchange the words "right" and "left" in the above directions.*

23 / LEG OVER

OBJECTIVE OF THE LEG OVER:
To trim inches from the waistline.

Important

In Fig. 76 the leg is placed as high toward the head as possible. Both shoulders must remain on the floor.

Practice Information

Perform three times on each side, alternating the sides, left-right. Hold each stretch for 10.

FIG. 74—*Lying on your back, stretch arms outward and bring your left knee as close to your chest as possible.*

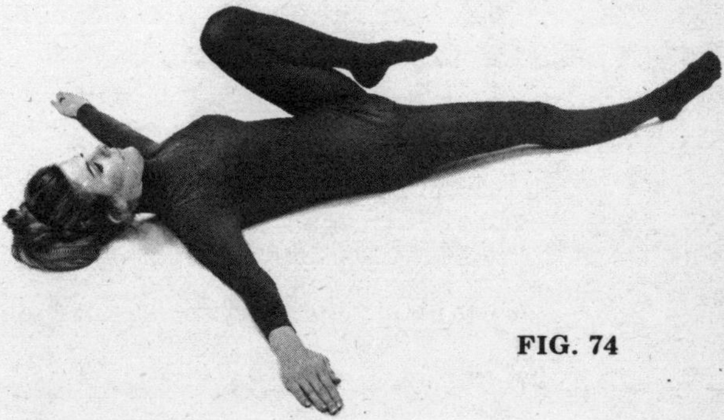

FIG. 74

FIG. 75

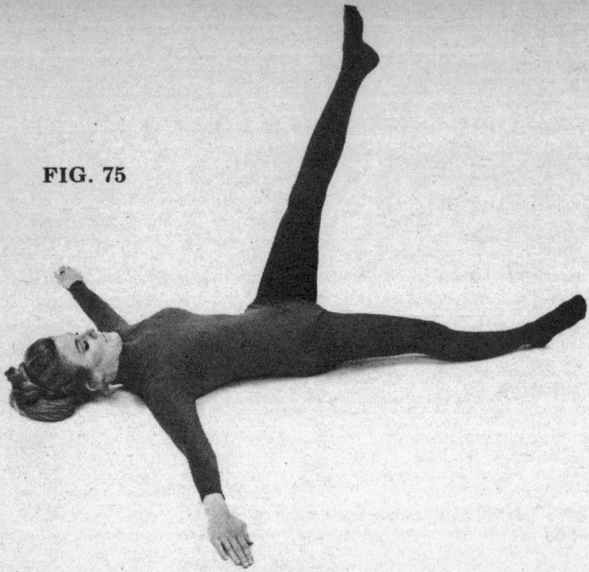

FIG. 76

FIG. 75—*Slowly straighten the leg.*

FIG. 76—*Slowly bring the leg over and down. Touch the floor. Hold for 10.*

Return the left·leg to the position of Fig. 75. Lower it to the floor.

Perform the identical movements with the right *leg.*

24 / PLOUGH *(Halasana)*

OBJECTIVE OF THE PLOUGH:

To provide an intensive concave stretch for the spine.

Important

Lower the legs very slowly in Figs. 78 and 79. Do not allow the legs to come "crashing" down against the floor. You should actually be able to feel the pressure shifting from the lower to the upper vertebrae as the legs are lowered. If you are unable to touch the floor, simply hold your extreme position for the count of 10. The holding will gradually work out the stiff vertebrae that are preventing you from completing the posture. The difficulty is in the spine, not the legs.

Practice Information

Perform twice. Hold your extreme position for 10.

Some students prefer to execute the extreme position of the Plough following the extreme position of the Shoulder Stand. This is simply a matter of placing the palms on the floor and slowly lowering your legs backward. (See the Shoulder Stand #12.)

FIG. 77

FIG. 78

FIG. 79

FIG. 77—*In a lying position push palms against floor and slowly raise legs.*

FIG. 78—*Push hard against the floor and swing your legs back over your head. Knees are straight. Slowly lower feet to floor.*

FIG. 79—*The completed posture. Toes rest on floor, chin is pressed tightly against upper chest. Knees are straight. Hold for 10. If this position is too difficult at present, simply lower the legs as far as possible without strain and hold your extreme position for 10.*

The movements for coming out of this posture are identical with those of the Shoulder Stand. Knees are brought down to forehead, trunk rolls forward slowly, neck is arched to keep back of head on floor, legs are straightened upright as in Fig. 77 and slowly lowered to floor. Relax in Deep Relaxation Posture.

25 / HEAD STAND *(Sirsasana)*

OBJECTIVES OF THE HEAD STAND:

To improve the faculties of the brain by activating the nerve centers; to maintain alertness of mind and help prevent hardening of the arteries; to improve the complexion and the condition of the scalp and hair; to help maintain good vision and hearing.

For many years past, mention of the word "Yoga" in the western world immediately evoked the image of the Head Stand posture. Although the study of Hatha Yoga has always included the many asanas we are learning in this book, it was the Head Stand that invariably received the notoriety. This was due to the fact that nothing appeared more bizarre or foreign to those who lacked any real knowledge of Yoga than a human being purposefully turning himself upside down. The entire subject of Yoga and the many wonderful physical and mental benefits that it offers were frequently dismissed with a remark such as: "Yogi? Oh yes, those funny fellows who stand on their heads. They must be crazy!" Not many people took the trouble to learn *why* gurus had been instructing their students in the Head Stand posture for several thousand years.

In recent years, however, the widespread interest and instruction in Europe and America has acquainted much of the general public with the therapeutic values of the asanas, including those of the Head Stand. Inverting the body for several minutes is now understood to be so practical and beneficial that I would venture to say it is undertaken by many tens of thousands of persons each day. We see an ever increasing number of photographs in our newspapers and periodicals of familiar public figures performing the Head Stand.

The student will, of course, recognize an obvious similarity between the Shoulder Stand, already learned, and the Head Stand. But whereas the Shoulder Stand cuts off the blood, to a great extent, at the neck (directing it into the thyroid), the Head Stand permits the free flow of the blood into the head. As such, the increased nourishment has a most positive effect on the brain, scalp, hair, complexion, vision and hearing.

Many beginners have reservations with regard to their ability in maintaining the required balance. But here the Head Stand is instructed in easy stages, over an extended period of time, enabling the student to perform as much or as little of this posture as he wishes. Important benefits can be derived from the most elementary of the positions. You may be pleasantly surprised at your "ability," regardless of age or background, if you patiently follow the directions.

Important

Bringing your knees as close to the chest as possible will enable you to transfer your balance more easily. If you find the position of Fig. 84 too difficult, simply hold that of Fig. 83 for thirty to sixty seconds. (Bringing the blood into the head will be beneficial even in the most modified of positions.) If you lose your balance in Fig. 84, attempt the position three times, then try again on the following day. If you continue to roll *forward* from the position of Fig. 84, use the wall for support by placing your pillow about six inches from the wall before beginning. Do not attempt to straighten your legs into the completed Head Stand at this time. You must first gain complete control and confidence in the Modified position.

Practice Information

Perform once. If you can attain the position of Fig. 84, begin by holding for ten seconds and gradually work up to three minutes. This can take several weeks or even months depending on how comfortable you feel in the posture.

If Fig. 84 is too difficult, perform the position of Fig. 83 once, beginning with thirty to sixty seconds and gradually adding seconds until a count of three minutes is reached. However, continue to attempt the Modified position from time to time.

FIG. 80

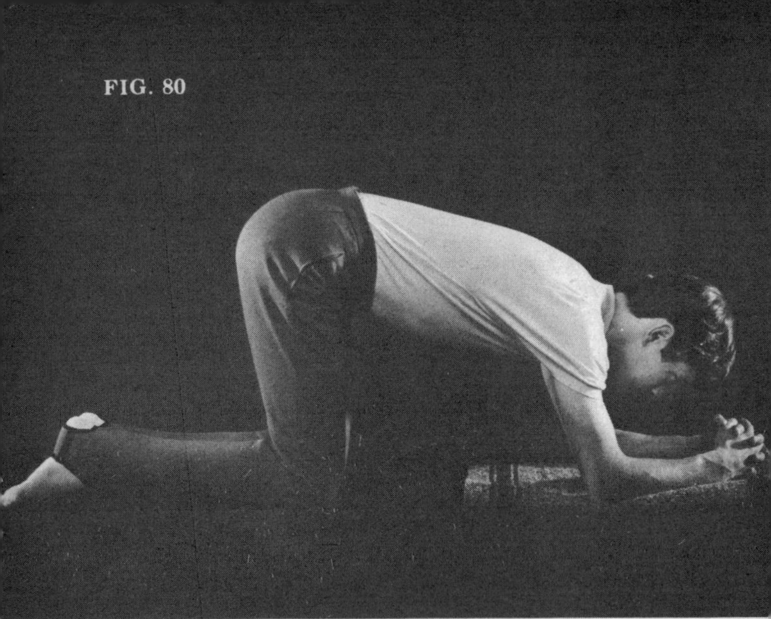

FIG. 80—*Place a small pillow or folded mat beneath your head.*

Sit on your heels.

Interlace your fingers and place your arms on the floor as illustrated.

FIG. 81—*Rest the top of your head on the mat; the back of your head is cradled firmly in your clasped hands.*

FIG. 82—*Place your toes on the floor and push up so that your body forms an arch.*

FIG. 81

FIG. 82

FIG. 83

FIG. 83 — *Walk forward on your toes and move your knees as close to your chest as possible.*

FIG. 84 — *Push off the floor lightly with your toes and transfer your weight so that it is evenly distributed between your head and forearms. This is the Modified Head Stand. Do not attempt to straighten your legs at this time. Hold for 10.*

Slowly lower your feet and knees to the floor. Remain with your head down for thirty to sixty seconds.

FIG. 84

26 / ALTERNATE NOSTRIL BREATHING
(Sahita Pranayama).

OBJECTIVES OF ALTERNATE NOSTRIL BREATHING:

To quiet and stabilize the mind and emotions; to aid in opening blocked nasal passages.

This is the second major breathing technique that we will learn and use. Our first technique, the Complete Breath, is designed to fill the lungs in their entirety and increase the supply of prana, life force. Very little need be added as to the merits of complete breathing. If you have been practicing as advised you are, at this point, well aware of the difference that can be experienced in every aspect of your life through the Complete Breath. Alternate Nostril Breathing will be equally meaningful. It is presented here primarily as a natural method for *tranquilizing* and its effect on the emotions and nervous tension is immediate.

A fascinating and highly esoteric theory of Hatha Yoga (one that you will be able to test for yourself) is that the nostrils are not the same; their functions differ. They interact in a positive-negative relationship analogous to that which is inherent throughout the physical world. The nostrils exist in this positive-negative structure so that the air that flows through them may be converted, regulated and balanced in a positive-negative ratio. If an imbalance exists, that is, if due to some fault of the nostrils or the breathing process, the positive-negative ratio is uneven, the Yogi contends that physical, emotional and mental illnesses can result. To help preserve the proper ratio or to restore the balance when necessary, Alternate Nostril Breathing is introduced. This very deliberate directing of the breath's flow through the nostrils in an alternate fashion has a most pronounced effect with regard to quieting the emotions and the mind. Therefore, the technique can be successfully utilized at any time when such disturbances are experienced.

In more advanced Yoga, for which this book can be considered a preparation, Alternate Nostril Breathing is employed to heighten inner awareness and acts as an excellent prelude to meditation.

Important

The finger position must be correct. Hand is relaxed, eyes remain closed throughout the exercise. It is essential to count in a steady, rhythmic manner. Start a metronomic beat going in your mind and have the breathing movements conform to it. Practice to make your breathing deep and as quiet as possible (air should not "hiss" in and out of the nostril.)

Practice Information

Perform five rounds as a part of your regular practice routine or whenever required to quiet mental or emotional disturbances. In cases of the latter it is necessary to seclude yourself for several minutes as soon as possible after these disturbances arise and perform at least five rounds. More may be done as necessary. It is best not to practice this or any of the Yoga techniques in the presence of other persons.

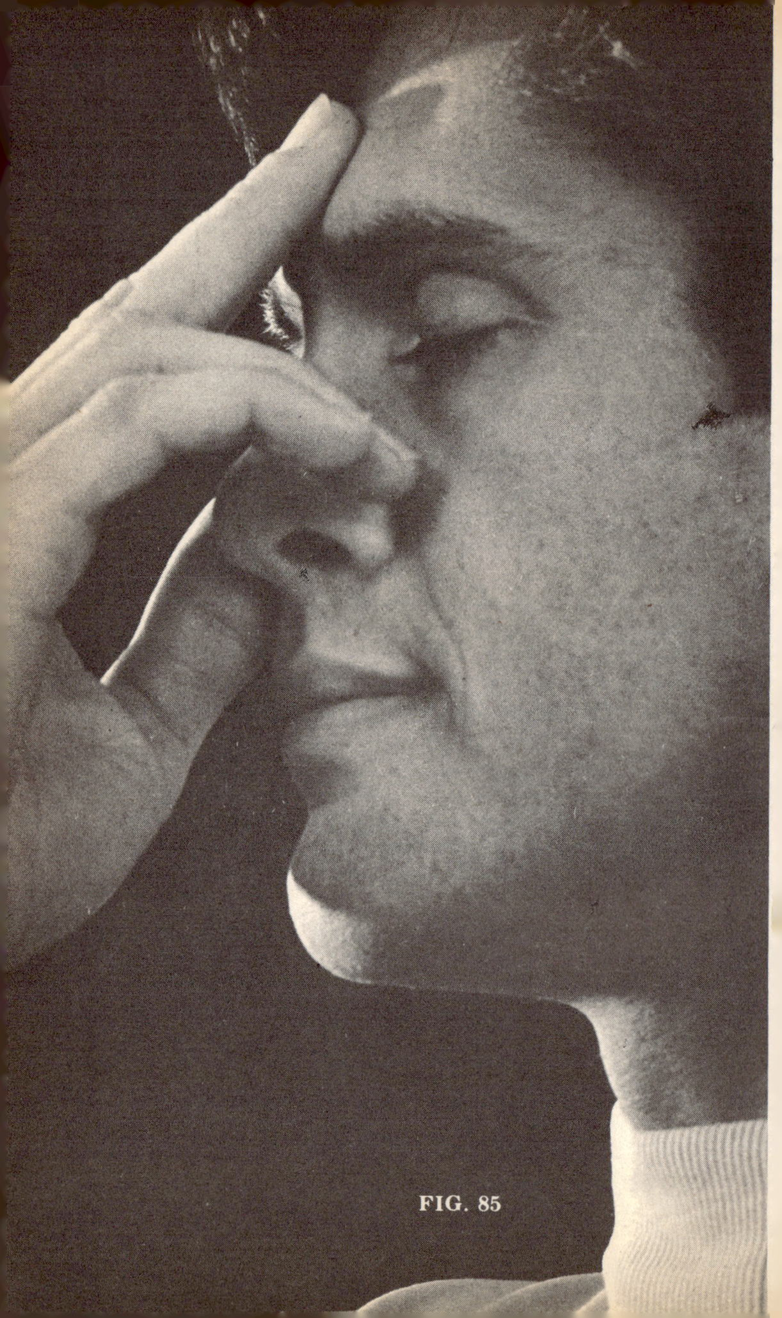

FIG. 85

FIG. 86

FIG. 85—*Study the illustration and place your right hand as depicted. The index and middle fingers rest lightly between the eyebrows. The thumb rests lightly against the right nostril and the ring finger against the left. The exercise is best performed in a cross-legged posture with your eyes closed.*

FIG. 86—*Execute a deep, slow, quiet exhalation through both nostrils.*

Press the thumb against the right nostril to close it.

Execute a deep, slow, quiet inhalation through your left nostril. Attempt to do this in a rhythmic count of 8 beats.

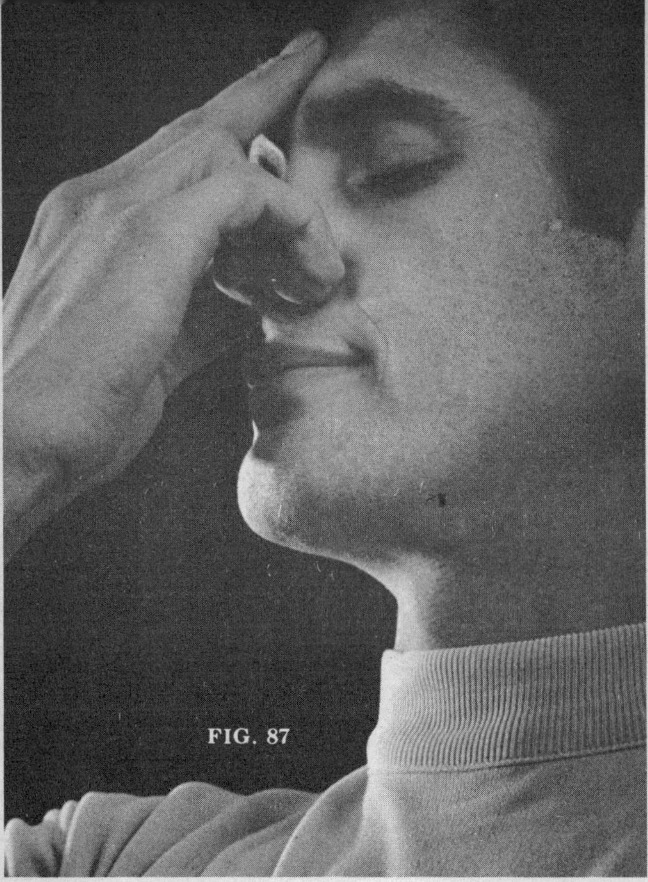

FIG. 87—*Press the left nostril closed with your ring finger. Both nostrils are now closed. Retain the air for a count of 4.*

FIG. 88—*Open the* right *nostril. Execute a deep, slow, quiet exhalation through the right nostril during a rhythmic count of 8. The left nostril remains closed.*

Keep the left nostril closed. When the exhalation is completed, immediately begin a deep, slow, quiet inhalation through the right *nostril in a rhythmic count of 8.*

Close the right nostril (both nostrils are now closed) and retain the air for a rhythmic count of 4.

Open the left *nostril (the right remains closed) and execute a deep, slow, quiet exhalation through the left nostril in a rhythmic count of 8.*

Keep the right nostril closed. When the exhalation is completed, you have returned to the original starting point and this completes one round *of the exercise. Without pause execute a deep, slow, quiet inhalation through the* left *nostril in a rhythmic count of 8. Continue the procedure as described above.*

Here is a summary of the procedure:

exhale deeply through both nostrils	
inhale through the left	*— count 8*
close both nostrils and retain	*— count 4*
exhale through the right	*— count 8*
inhale through the right	*— count 8*
close both nostrils and retain	*— count 4*
exhale through the left	*— count 8*
repeat	

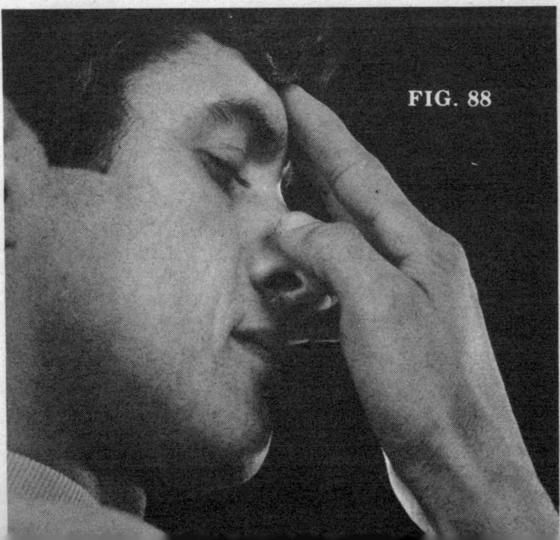

FIG. 88

THE FIVE-POSTURE ROUTINE

The following five postures are composed of simple movements. However, they are highly effective for exercising and stimulating areas of the body that are frequently neglected. You will note that the movements begin with the scalp and work down through the eyes, face, neck, shoulders and chest. All areas of the body are interconnected. A headache may be caused by flat feet and tension in the neck can come from stiffness in the base of the spine. It is therefore our intention to exercise *every* area of the body; to remove tension at each point where it may lodge, to promote good blood circulation wherever it may grow poor, to impart firmness and tone to *all* muscles, etc. Only this *whole* approach to physical fitness can be considered, in the Yogic view, as valid. Hence the need for the five little techniques that follow. The entire routine can be done within approximately five minutes or less and, requiring so little time, should be undertaken daily. Many students do these five exercises, in addition to some complete breathing upon arising, to help the body wake up quickly.

27 / SCALP EXERCISE

OBJECTIVES OF THE SCALP EXERCISE:

To stimulate the scalp and improve the condition of the hair.

Important

Don't be too gentle. Pull hard so that the scalp tingles.

Practice Information

Perform forward and backward 25 times. There is no "hold" in this exercise.

FIG. 89 —*Reach down into the roots of your hair with both hands and firmly grasp as much of it as possible.*

FIG. 90 —*Pull down firmly, making the scalp move forward as far as possible.*

Without pause pull up making the scalp move backward as far as possible.

Without pause repeat.

FIG. 89

FIG. 90

28 / LION

OBJECTIVES OF THE LION:

To firm muscles of the face, chin and neck.

Important

No massage, cream, lotion or machine can restore muscle tone to your face and neck. This is an *internal* matter; firmness and good circulation in these areas must come from within, from muscular movements. The extension of the tongue in the Lion posture will provide this movement.

Don't be afraid to extend the tongue far out and make a ferocious face (like a lion). The farther the tongue is extended, the more firming that will transpire in the face and neck. If you do not feel an intensive stretching in your neck, the tongue is not being sufficiently extended. Keep your eyes wide open during the stretch. This will often reduce wrinkles and crow's feet in that area. Also spread the fingers as wide apart as possible to strengthen them.

Settle back very slowly following the stretch.

Practice Information

Perform five times. Hold each stretch for 15.

FIG. 91 —*Sit on your heels, hands rest on knees.*

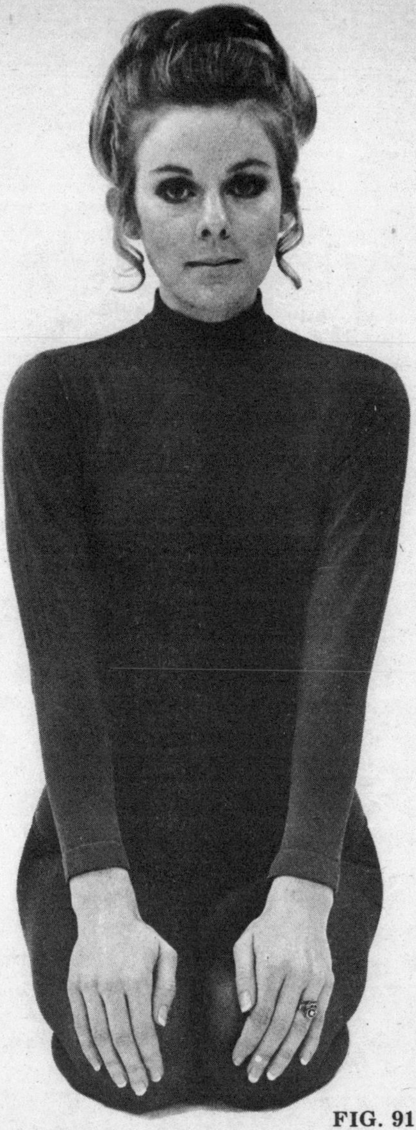

FIG. 91

FIG. 92

FIG. 92 — *Tense all muscles. Move trunk forward. Widen eyes, spread fingers. Extend tongue as far out and down as possible. This is a very intensive movement and you must feel all the muscles of your neck working. Hold for 15. Do not relax the tongue.*

Very slowly withdraw the tongue, relax all muscles and settle back onto your heels. Relax a few moments. Repeat.

29 / NECK EXERCISE

OBJECTIVE OF THE NECK EXERCISE:

To remove tension throughout the neck.

Important

Note the emphasis on extreme *slow motion*. The head does not simply turn. It rolls in an exaggerated fashion to each of the extreme positions. Eyes are closed for relaxation.

Practice Information

Perform four times in all. Roll counter-clockwise (to the left) then clockwise (to the right). Repeat. Hold each stretch for 10.

Perform whenever necessary to relieve tension in the neck.

FIG. 93—*In a seated posture slowly lower your head so that your chin rests against your chest. Hold for 10. Eyes should be closed.*

FIG. 93

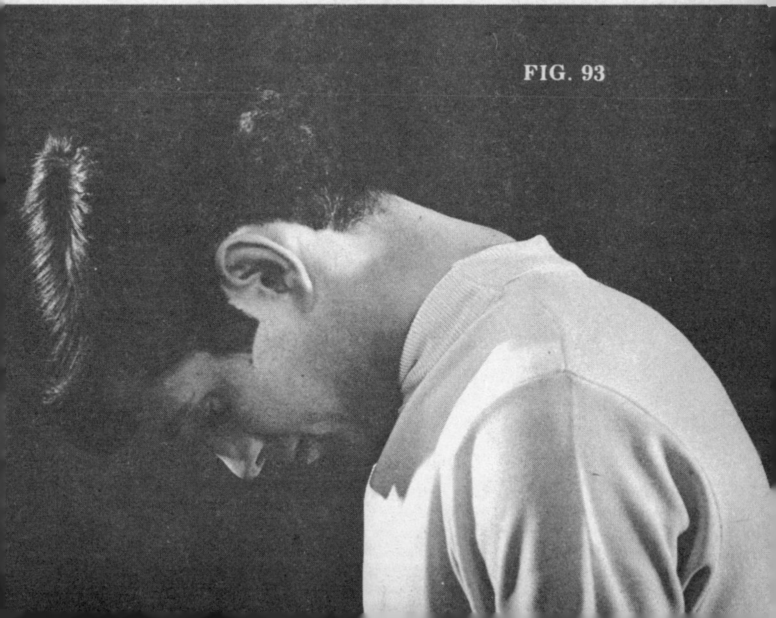

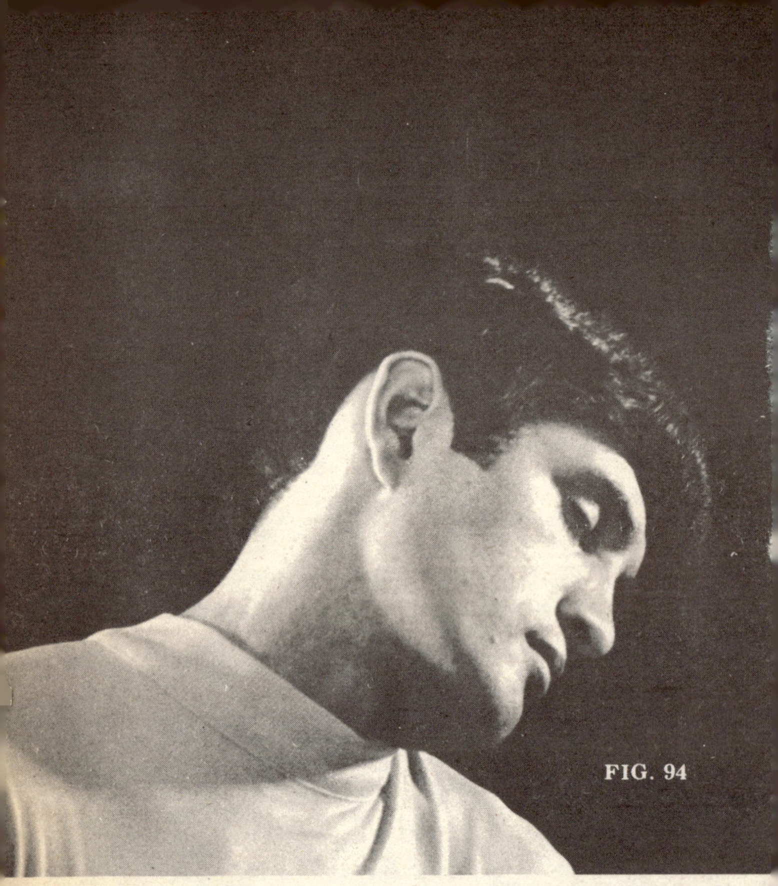

FIG. 94

FIG. 94—*In very slow motion roll your head to the extreme left position. Hold for 10.*

In very slow motion roll your head to the extreme backward position. Hold for 10.

In very slow motion roll your head to the extreme right position. Hold for 10.

In very slow motion roll your head to the forward position of Fig. 93. Hold for 10.

Repeat the movements but now roll in a clockwise *manner, i.e., to the extreme right. Hold for 10. Continue to the backward position, etc.*

30 / POSTURE EXERCISE

OBJECTIVES OF THE POSTURE EXERCISE:

To loosen the shoulders and "set" them up and back.

Important

The arms need move no more than a few inches in both directions. If your hands will not meet behind your back, hold the ends of a rope or a handkerchief. This exercise moves the shoulders in a very special and beneficial way and should not be neglected.

Practice Information

Perform five times. Hold each of the up and down pulls for 10.

This is another excellent exercise for sedentary workers, especially those who spend most of their workday at a desk. It has also proved beneficial in certain cases of bursitis.

FIG. 95—*In a seated posture place the back of your left hand against your back with the palm facing away.*

Bring your right arm over your right shoulder and lock the fingers as illustrated.

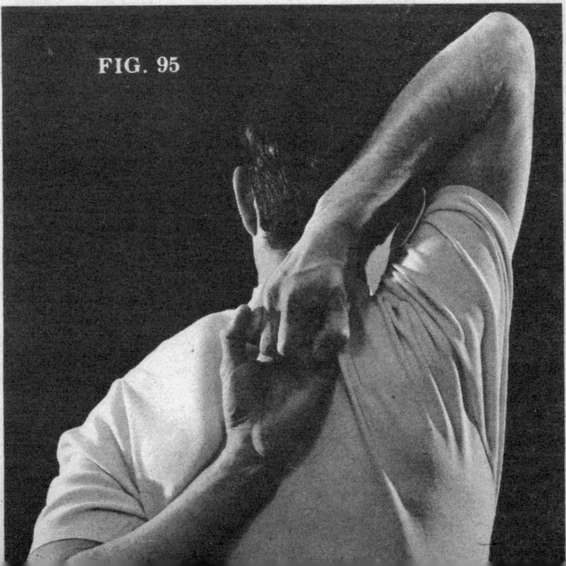

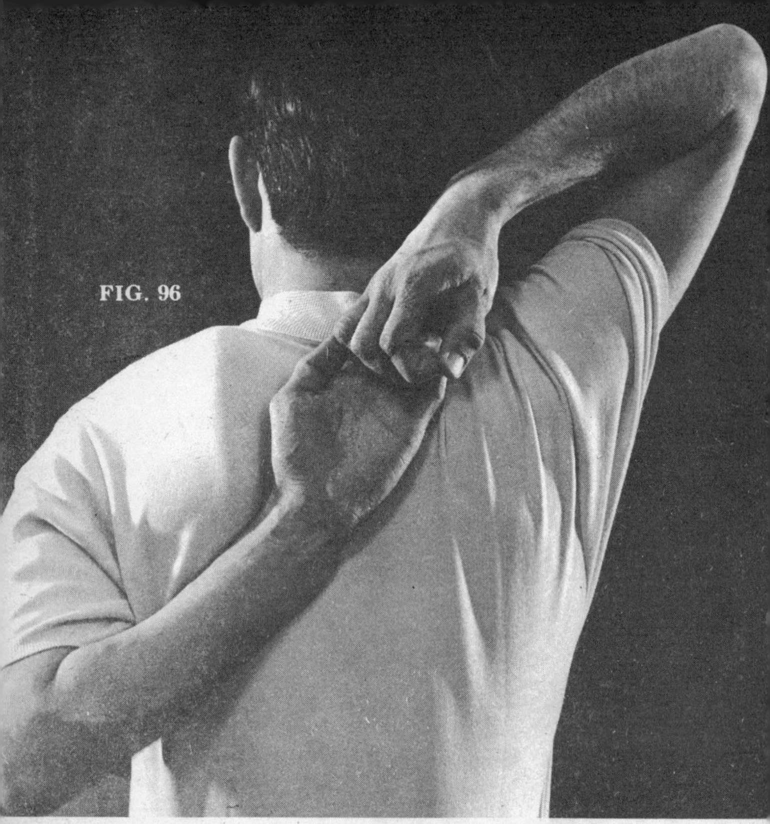

FIG. 96 —*Pull up with the right hand so that both arms are raised an inch or two (Fig. 96). Hold for 10.*

Pull down with the left hand so that both arms are lowered an inch or two. Hold for 10.

Repeat the up-down movements.

31 /BUST EXERCISE

OBJECTIVES OF THE BUST EXERCISE:
To develop and firm the chest and bust.

Practice Information

Perform five times. Hold each raise for 10.

FIG. 97—*In a seated posture interlace your fingers behind your back.*

FIG. 97

FIG. 98

FIG. 98 —*In very slow motiòn raise your arms as high as possible. Keep the trunk erect. Hold for 10.*

Slowly lower your arms. Relax a moment. Repeat.

INTERMEDIATE SECTION

Use of this section need not wait until all of the postures of the Elementary Section are perfected. Your progress in Hatha Yoga will not be in a straight line. That is to say, there will be days when you make excellent progress, but this may be followed by a short period during which there is a "setback." Your body temporarily "contracts" in a manner that enables it to "set" itself into the new physical patterns it has been learning. When this period of contraction and setting is completed, you will once again be able to move ahead. If you understand that the normal progress in this study consists of several strides forward, followed by one backward, you will never be discouraged when you experience what appears to be a setback; rather, you will practice very easily and patiently until you have worked through this period.

Since the organism of each student reacts differently to the various postures, that is, since some people find themselves weak, stiff, tense or underdeveloped in certain areas and other people find this to be the case in different areas, it is impossible to predict, *en masse,* at what point the intermediate material should be introduced. Each student will become proficient in certain postures earlier than in others. For example, some are able to perform the completed Plough and Cobra postures, as presented in the Elementary Section, in their very first attempts. But these same students find great difficulty with the Lotus or Bow. The rule, then, for the use of this Intermediate Section, is: Whenever you have mastered the final positions of the Elementary Section and your organism remains comfortable in these final positions *for a period of two weeks of practice*, you may move into the intermediate movements of those postures. Remember to test yourself carefully for the two-week period; if you jump the gun and undertake the more advanced work prior to this, you may actually retard your progress.

In addition to the intermediate movements, the points that distinguish the Intermediate from the Elementary section are: (1) longer "holding" intervals in certain postures; (2) the fixing of the consciousness fully on all of the movements and not allowing the mind to wander. You must now become acutely aware of what is happening in your organism, especially during the holding periods. You must *feel* the stretching, *feel* the stimulation, *feel* the relaxation. This practice of deep concentration on all movements results in a pronounced increase in the effectiveness of the exercises.

FULL-LOTUS *(Padmasana)*

Continued from Exercise #2, page 16

To practice for the Full-Lotus, obtain a pillow which provides six to twelve inches of height. When you sit on this pillow the additional height often enables the knees to be lowered to the floor. Once either knee can touch the floor without aid from the hands, the Full-Lotus may be accomplished.

Important

This is the classical meditation posture and is worthy of the most patient practice. It will be necessary for either knee to touch the floor (Fig. 99) to execute the Full-Lotus. If this is not yet possible, simply place either foot on either thigh (Fig. 99), rest your arm on your knee and remain in this position for approximately two minutes. Then reverse the legs and hold for an additional two minutes. This light pressure of the arm will aid in gradually lowering the knee to the floor. You must be patient; this is an advanced posture.

Practice Information

The first time you are able to successfully execute the Full-Lotus on either side, hold the position for no longer than 30 seconds. Add approximately 15 seconds in each practice session until you can retain for five minutes and longer. Assume the Full-Lotus for all exercises where a "cross-legged" posture is stipulated. The advanced practice of meditation often requires the Full-Lotus for fifteen to thirty minutes.

FIG. 99

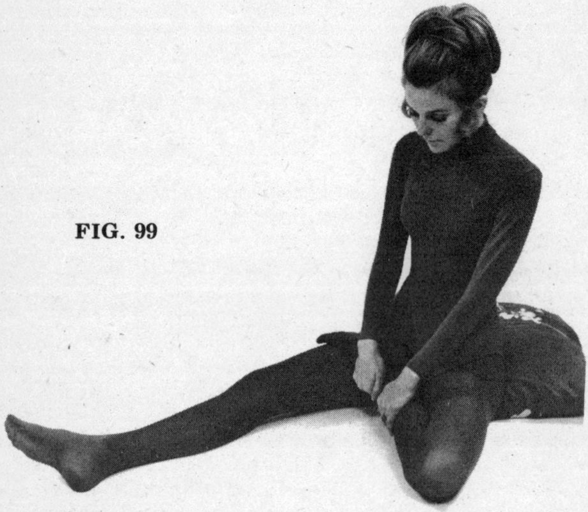

FIG. 99—*Seated on the pillow place your left foot as high as possible on the right thigh.*

FIG. 100—*Place your right foot on top of the left thigh. Assume the hand position (*mudra*) depicted in Fig. 101. Trunk is erect but relaxed. Eyelids are lowered, not completely closed.*

FIG. 101—*A closeup of the mudra. Note that the top of the index finger is pressed* firmly *against the thumb.*

FIG. 100

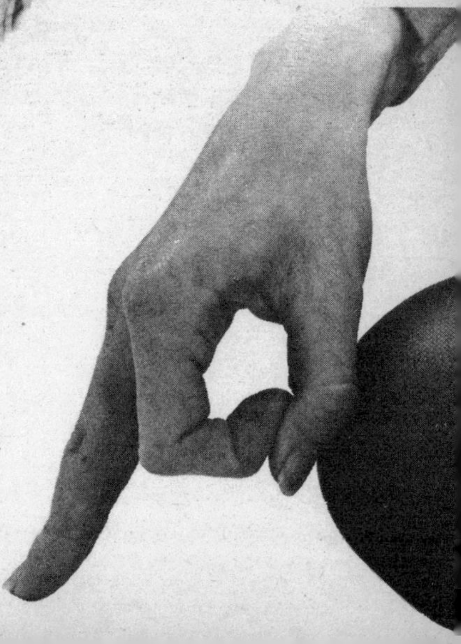

FIG. 101

FIG. 102

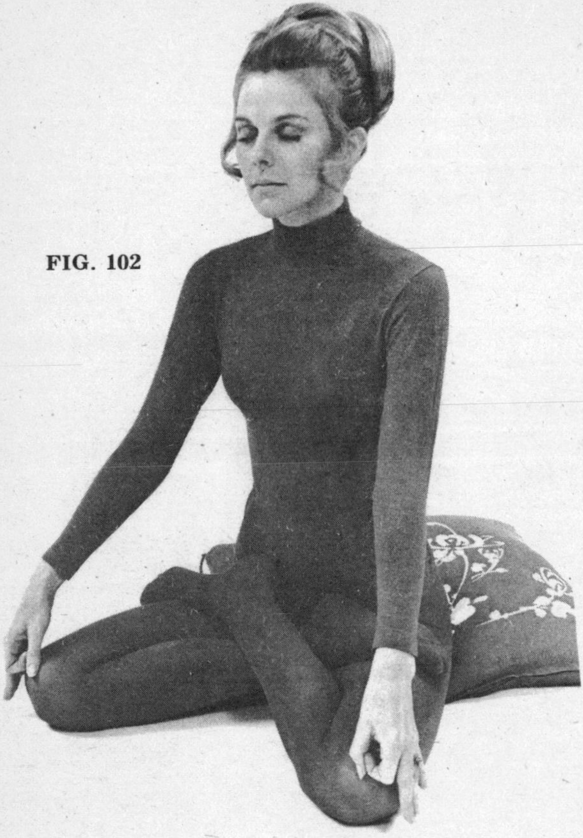

FIG. 102—*Attempt the Full-Lotus with the legs reversed. Some students find the reversed position easier, due to the structure of the legs.*

BACK STRETCH

Continued from Exercise #4, page 25

Practice Information

Perform the calves, ankles, feet and advanced position with the elbows lowered once each. Hold each stretch for 10. Remember to *feel* what is happening in your organism through the various stretches; do not allow your consciousness to wander. If you find your mind is running away from the stretching, bring it back, gently but firmly.

Refer to Figs. 8-12.

FIG. 103—*Raise your arms as previously (in slow motion, with poise and balance) and now bend backward as far as possible.* Feel the firming of the abdomen.

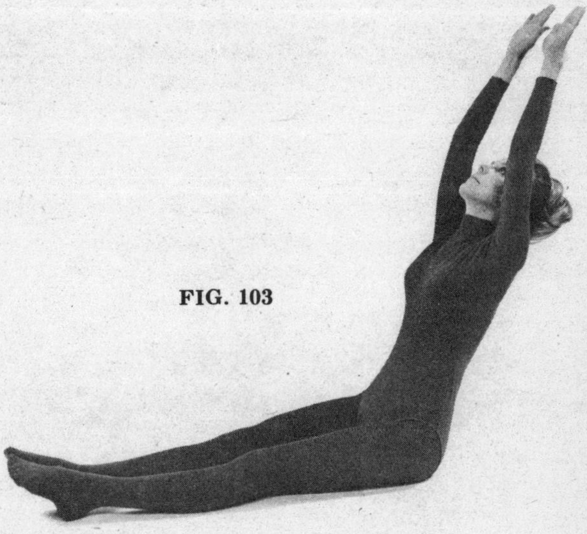

FIG. 103

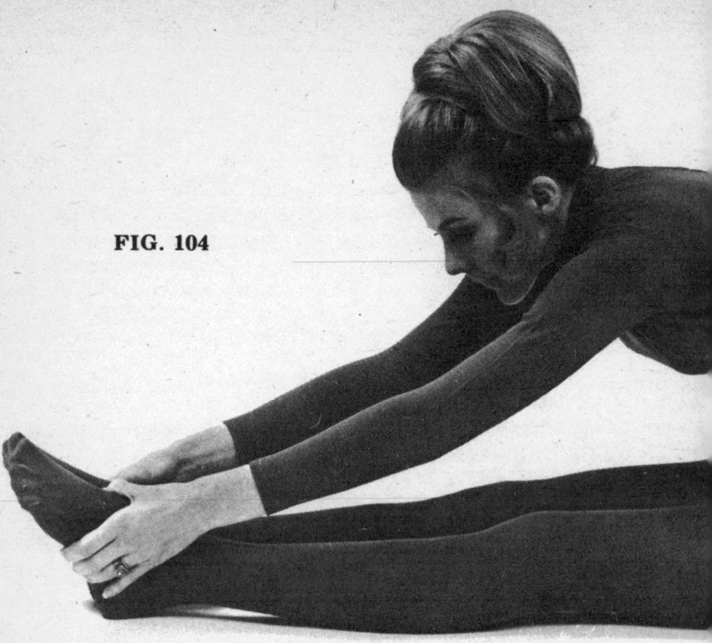

FIG. 104

FIG. 105

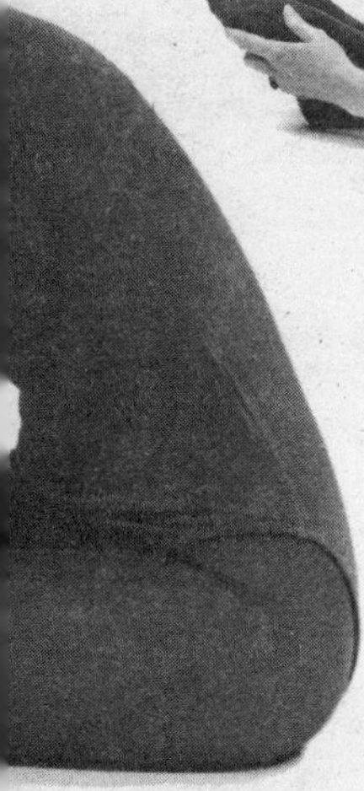

FIG. 106

FIG. 104—*Come forward slowly. If you will "rock" or "sway" very gently from side to side as you bend forward, you will help to loosen the spine.*

Take a firm hold on your feet.

FIG. 105—*Pull your trunk downward and rest your forehead on your knees. Hold without motion for 10.* Feel *the stretch.*

FIG. 106—*This is the most advanced position. It provides maximum stretching for the back and should be attempted only after you are comfortable in the position of Fig. 105. Lower both elbows to touch the floor. Hold for 10.* Feel *the intensive stretching.*

Very slowly raise your trunk to the upright position. Relax.

CHEST EXPANSION

Continued from Exercise #5, page 30

Practice Information

Perform the moderate stretch of Figs. 15 and 16 once and the extreme stretch, including the leg movements instructed above, once. Hold the backward stretches for 5 and the forward stretches, including those of the legs for 10. Remember to *experience* the stretching.

FIG. 107

FIG. 108

FIG. 107—*Perform the movements of Figs. 13 and 14. Now, very cautiously, bend as far backward as possible. Be careful not to strain. Fig. 107 depicts the most advanced backward movement. Hold for 5.* Feel *the stretching.*

FIG. 108—*Very slowly bend as far forward as possible. Fig. 108 depicts the most advanced forward bend. Hold for 10.* Feel *the stretch.*

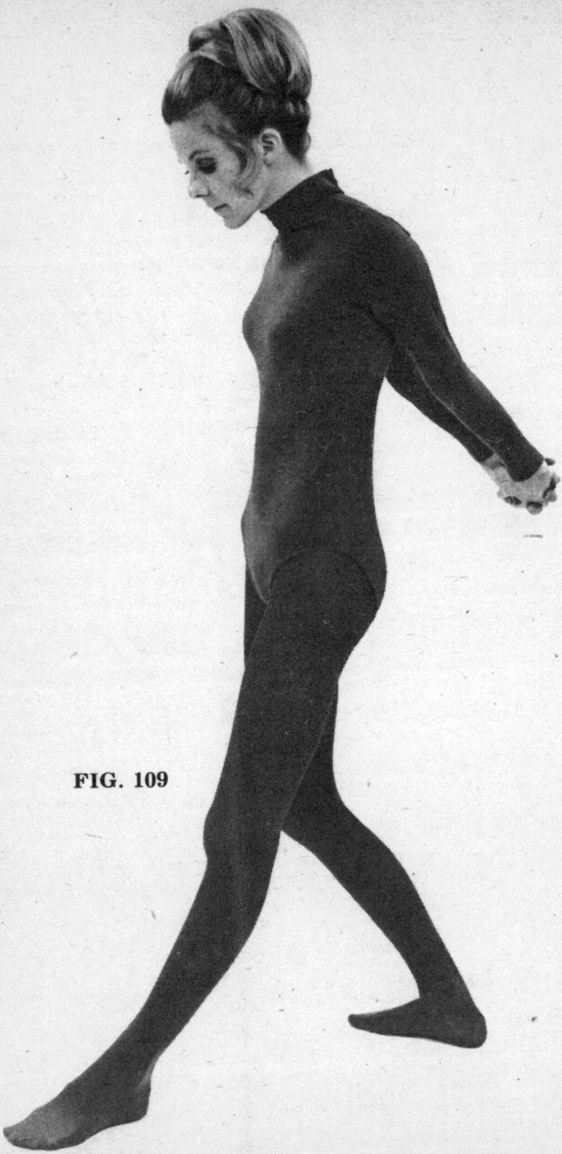

FIG. 109

FIG. 109—*Raise your trunk high enough to extend your left leg approximately two feet to the front and side.*

FIG. 110—*Twist your trunk to the left and lower your forehead as close to the knee as possible. Right knee bends to aid in lowering the trunk. Hold for 10. This movement is primarily for the "ham string" muscles of the backs of the thighs.* Feel *the stretching at that point.*

Very slowly raise your trunk high enough to draw the left leg in and to extend the right foot.

Perform the identical movements to the right knee. Hold for 10.

Slowly straighten to the upright position. Draw the right leg in, lower arms to your sides and relax.

FIG. 110

FIG. 111

COBRA

Continued from Exercise #6, page 34

Important

The raising and lowering of the trunk without the aid of the hands greatly strengthens the lumbar area. When the arms are brought forward in raising and backward in lowering, the movements are graceful and smooth as in a slow motion swimming stroke. In Fig. 113 your head must be very far back, elbows straight, legs relaxed. The "hold" is now increased to a count of 20. The "twisting" movements impart additional flexibility to the spine.

FIG. 112

Practice Information

Perform once in the Modified position as learned previously (Figs. 17-20) and hold the raised position for 10. Perform once as directed above and hold the raised position for 20 and the twisting movements for 10 each.

FIG. 111—*Refer to Figs. 17 and 18. Now, as you begin to raise your head, your arms remain at the sides. Raise your trunk slowly, as high as possible,* without the aid of your hands.

FIG. 112—*When the trunk has been raised as high as possible, gracefully and smoothly bring the hands up from the sides and place them beneath the shoulders as we have done previously.*

FIG. 113

FIG. 114

FIG. 113—*In very slow motion continue to raise your trunk with the hands now pushing against the floor. Your head bends far backward and your spine is continually curved.*

Fig. 113 depicts the completed posture. Compare with the previous completed posture of Fig. 20. Your trunk is now several inches higher and your elbows are now straight. Hold for 20. Feel *the stretching.*

FIG. 114—*Upon completion of the count, bend your* right *elbow (left elbow remains straight) and slowly twist your trunk as far to the left as possible. Attempt to see your left heel. Breathe normally. Hold for 10.* Feel *the twisting of the spine.*

FIG. 115

FIG. 115—*Slowly return the trunk to the extreme raised position of Fig. 113.*

Now bend your left elbow (right remains straight) and slowly twist as far to the right as possible. Attempt to see your right heel. Hold for 10. Feel *the twisting.*

Return to the position of Fig. 113.

Very slowly lower your trunk halfway to the floor. When this halfway position is reached, smoothly and gracefully bring your arms back to your sides so that your back muscles must work hard to support your trunk.

Continue to slowly lower your trunk until your forehead rests on the floor. Rest your cheek on the floor and allow the body to go completely limp. Experience *the deep relaxation.*

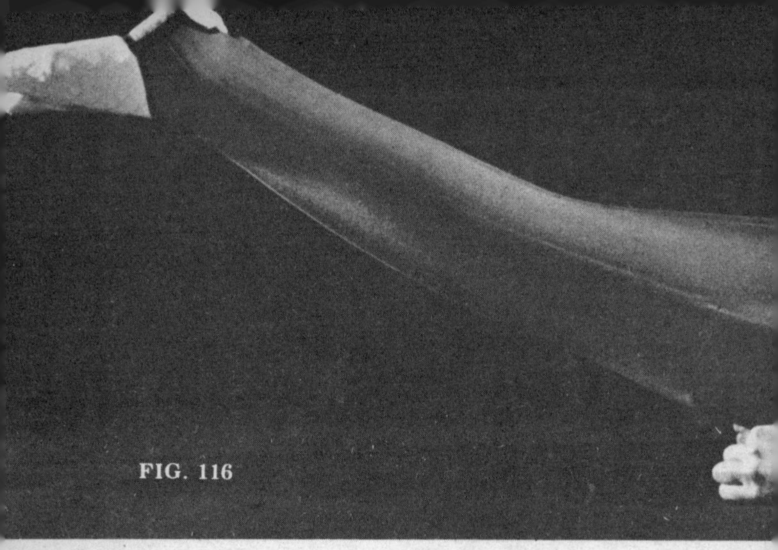

FIG. 116

LOCUST

Continued from Exercise #7, page 37

Practice Information

Perform once with the legs separately (Fig. 21), once in the moderate position, once in the extreme position and, if possible, once in the advanced position. Hold each raise for 10.

FIG. 116—*Refer to Figs. 21 and 22. We now attempt to raise the legs to this extreme position. The knees remain straight. Hold for 10.*

Slowly *lower the legs to the floor and simultaneously exhale. Rest your cheek on the floor and relax for several moments.*

FIG. 117—*This is an advanced and difficult position. It is introduced here as a challenge to the student for future practice. In this position the knees are bent to allow for the higher raise of the legs. Hold for 10. Lower as before. Relax completely.*

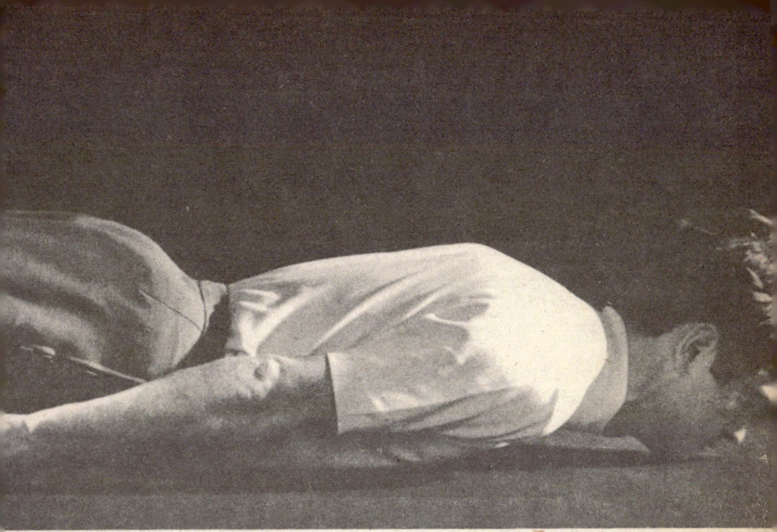

FIG. 117

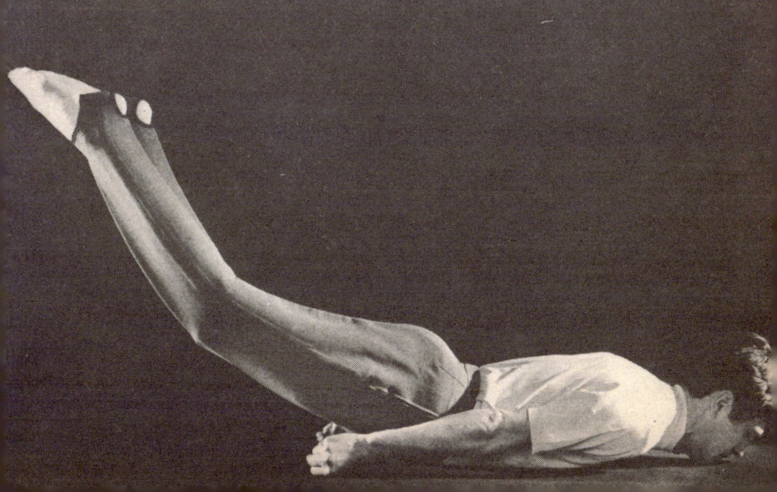

BOW

Continued from Exercise #8, page 40

Important

Remember to keep your knees close together. This intensifies the strengthening for the back. Head is back and eyes look up except in the forward rocking. *Feel* what is happening in your back.

FIG. 118

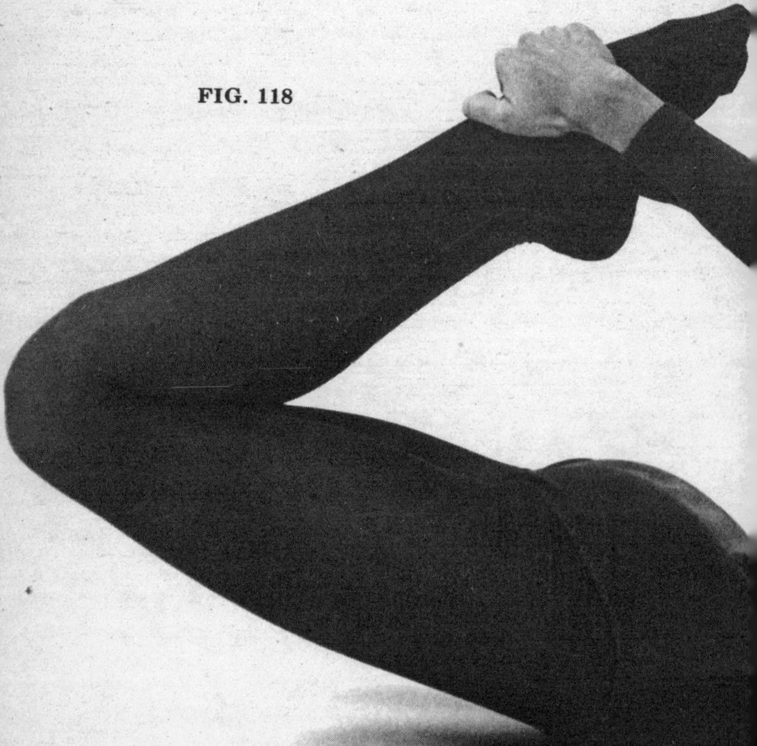

Practice Information

Perform the moderate position of Fig. 25 twice and the extreme position of Fig. 118 once. Hold each raise for 10. Perform the rocking movements five times in continuous slow motion.

FIG. 118—*Refer to Figs. 23-25. We now attempt to raise both the trunk and the knees to this extreme position. Your head is back and knees are held as close together as possible. Hold for 10.* Feel *the intensive stretching in the back.*

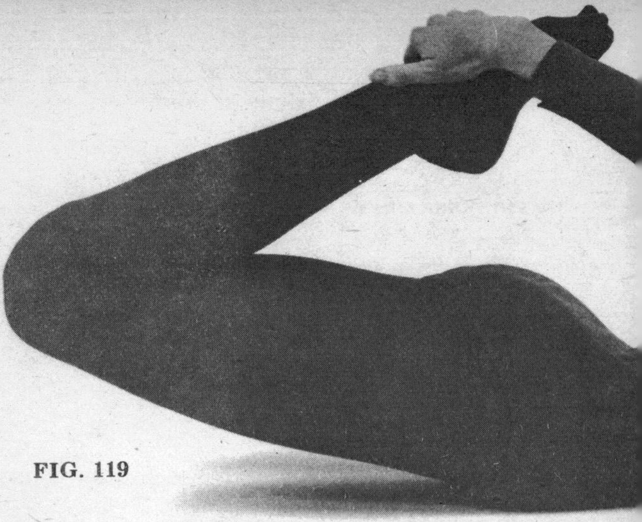

FIG. 119

FIG. 119 — *We will now attempt to "rock" forward, and backward on the abdomen in a hobby-horse movement. Upon completion of the count of 10 in Fig. 118, hold your feet firmly and rock* forward *bringing your chin as close to the floor as possible.*

FIG. 120 — *Without pause, rock* backward, *bringing the knees as close to the floor as possible. These movements should be performed smoothly, without "jerking."*

Without pause, repeat the forward-backward rocking movements.

FIG. 121 — *It is very important to come out of the posture as smoothly as possible. When the rocking movements are completed, return to the position of Fig. 118 and stop all motion for a moment. Now lower your knees to the floor first. Then slowly lower chin. Finally, release the feet and lower your legs slowly to the floor. Rest cheek on floor and relax completely.*

FIG. 120

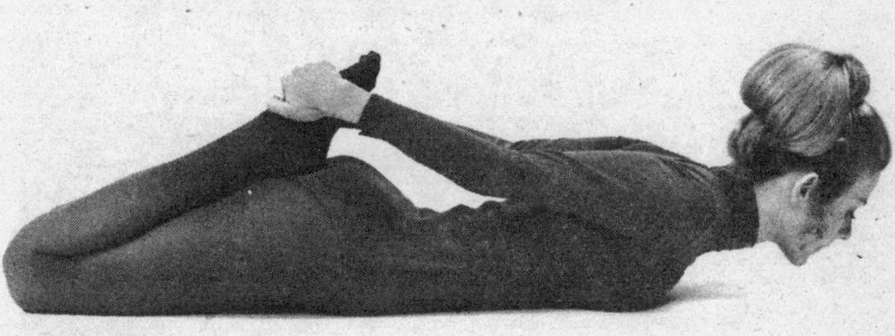

FIG. 121

SIDE BEND

Continued from Exercise #9, page 43

Practice Information

Perform in each of the three positions (Figs. 26, 27, 122) once. Hold each of the first two bends for 10 and the extreme bend for 15. Alternate the sides, i.e., left-right.

FIG. 122—*Refer to Figs. 26-28. Now we wish to execute this extreme position to the left. Arms remain parallel with each other and also with the floor. Head bends far to the left. Hold for 15.* Feel *the stretching and firming of the entire right side.*

FIG. 122

FIG. 123

FIG. 123—*Perform the identical movement to the right. Hold for 15.* Feel *the stretching and firming in the entire left side.*

Slowly straighten to the upright position.

Slowly lower your arms to the sides and relax.

TRIANGLE

Continued from Exercise #10, page 47

Practice Information

Perform once in the calf position, hold for 10. Perform once in the ankle position, hold for 15. Alternate the sides, left-right, left-right.

FIG. 124

FIG. 125

FIG. 124—*Refer to Figs. 29-32. Now assume the widest possible stance. Your legs should be approximately three feet apart. Arms are raised as previously.*

FIG. 125—*Slowly bend to the left and take a firm hold on your ankle. Neck is relaxed, head is down.*

FIG. 126

FIG. 126—*Pull on the ankle (elbow may bend) and lower the trunk as far as possible. The right arm is once again brought over your head so that it is parallel with the floor. Hold for 15.* Feel *the stretching in the upper thigh and throughout the right side.*

Slowly straighten to the position of Fig. 124.

Perform the identical movements to the right side. Hold for 15.

Slowly straighten to the position of Fig. 124. Gracefully lower arms to sides and draw legs together. Relax.

BACKWARD BEND

Continued from Exercise #11, page 50

Important

In these positions the toes and ankles are greatly strengthened. You must proceed cautiously, as your toes may be weak and must be gradually accustomed to supporting the weight you are now placing on them. Simply sitting in the position of Fig. 127 for one minute each time you practice will quickly strengthen the toes and ankles.

Practice Information

Perform once each in the positions of Figs. 35, 36, 129 and, when possible, Fig. 131. Hold each of the stretches for 10.

FIG. 127—*Refer to Figs. 33-36. Now change the position of the feet so that the toes rest on floor as illustrated. Sit back on your heels.*

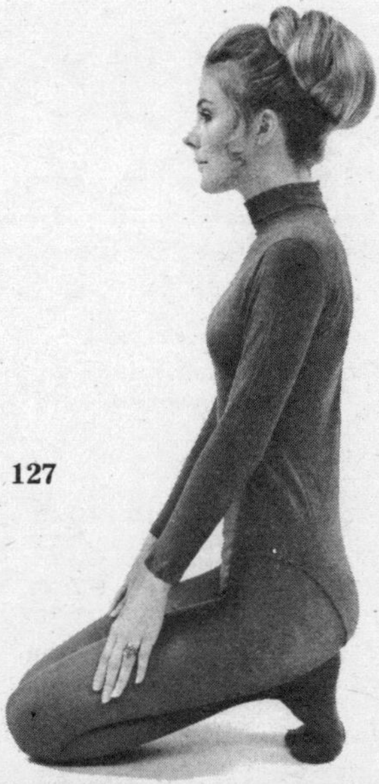

FIG. 127

FIG. 128

FIG. 128—*Cautiously inch backward on fingertips.*

FIG. 129—*Place palms firmly on floor as illustrated and perform the same stretching movement as previously (Fig. 36). Now, however, the trunk is higher due to the position of the feet. Note that the knees are together and the arms are even with the thighs. Fingers point away from you. Hold for 10.*

Slowly raise your head, inch forward on fingertips, return to position of Fig. 127 and come into a cross-legged posture. Relax.

FIG. 130—*This is a difficult and advanced position and, as with the advanced Locust, is introduced here as a challenge for future practice. The position of Fig. 130 will follow the extreme position of Fig. 129. When the count of 10 is completed, slowly raise your head several inches and lower either elbow very cautiously to the floor.*

Next, lower the other elbow to the floor. Hold your feet.

FIG. 131—*The completed advanced posture. Your hands hold your feet. Your head is very slowly and cautiously lowered to touch the floor as illustrated. Hold for 10. Relax all muscles as much as possible to make the hold easier.*

Very slowly raise your head several inches. Place either palm firmly on the floor. Push up so that you are able to slip the other palm against the floor. Now raise the trunk to the upright position and proceed to come into the cross-legged posture. Relax.

FIG. 129

FIG. 130

FIG. 131

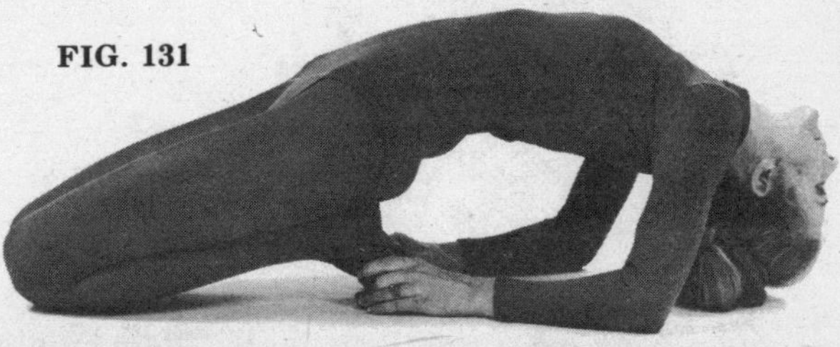

SHOULDER STAND

Continued from Exercise #12, page 54

Practice Information

Perform your extreme position once. Hold for one to five minutes. Perform the variations once, holding each for 20.

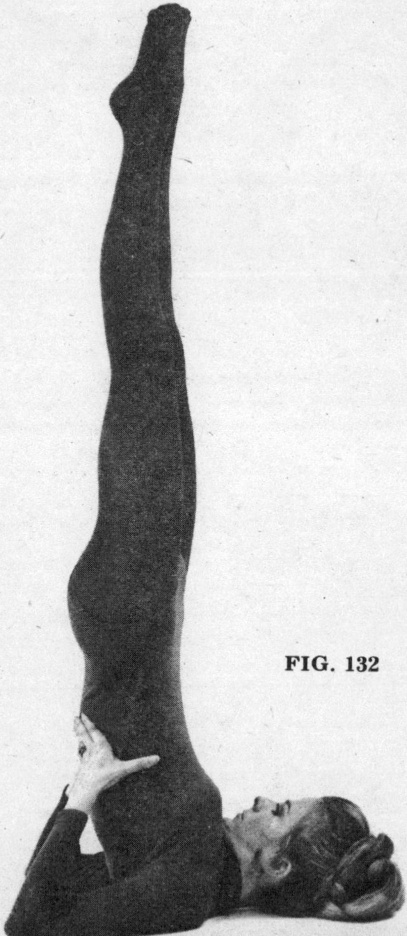

FIG. 132

FIG. 133

FIG. 132 — *This is the completed posture. When you are comfortable in the modified position of Fig. 39, slowly straighten your trunk and legs into this completely vertical position. Your trunk is now at a direct right angle with your head. The chin should be firmly pressed against the top of the chest. Body is straight, but relaxed. Hold for one to five minutes. During the hold, breathe as slowly as possible and attempt to fix your consciousness fully on the breathing. Do not let your mind wander.*

FIG. 133 — *These "variations" follow the completion of the one to five minute count.*

Very slowly separate the legs as far as possible and hold this position for 20.

FIG. 134

FIG. 134 — *Very slowly twist your trunk as far to the left as possible, holding the legs in their separated position. Actually, the legs are held stationary; it is the trunk that twists. Hold for 20.*

Hold the legs as they are and very slowly twist as far to the right as possible. Hold for 20.

Slowly return to the position of Fig. 133. Draw the legs together as in Fig. 132. Proceed to come out of the posture as previously directed.

SIDE RAISE

Continued from Exercise #13, page 59

Practice Information

Lying on the left side, perform the movements of Fig. 40 (the right leg only) once, Fig. 41 (moderate raise) once. Hold each raise for 10. Perform your extreme raise twice. Hold for 15. Perform the identical routine lying on the right side.

FIG. 135—*Refer to Figs. 40 and 41. Now we attempt to raise the legs to the higher position illustrated. Legs must remain together. Hold for 15. Concentrate on the movements.*

Slowly lower the legs to the floor and relax a few moments. Repeat.

FIG. 135

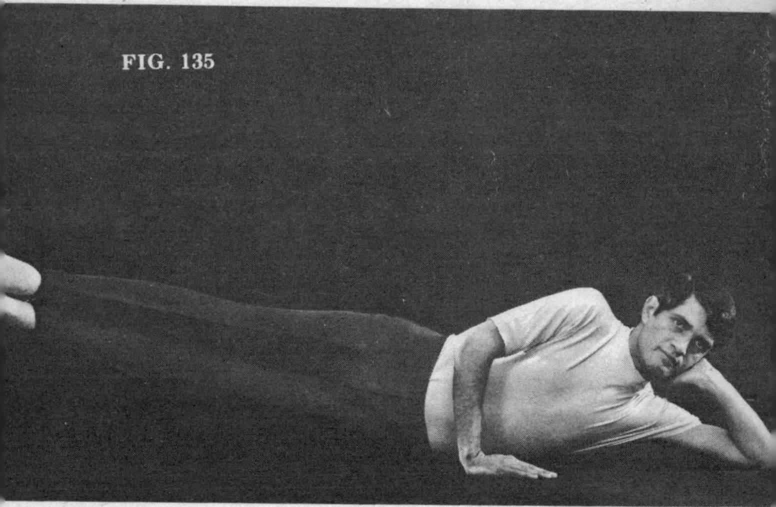

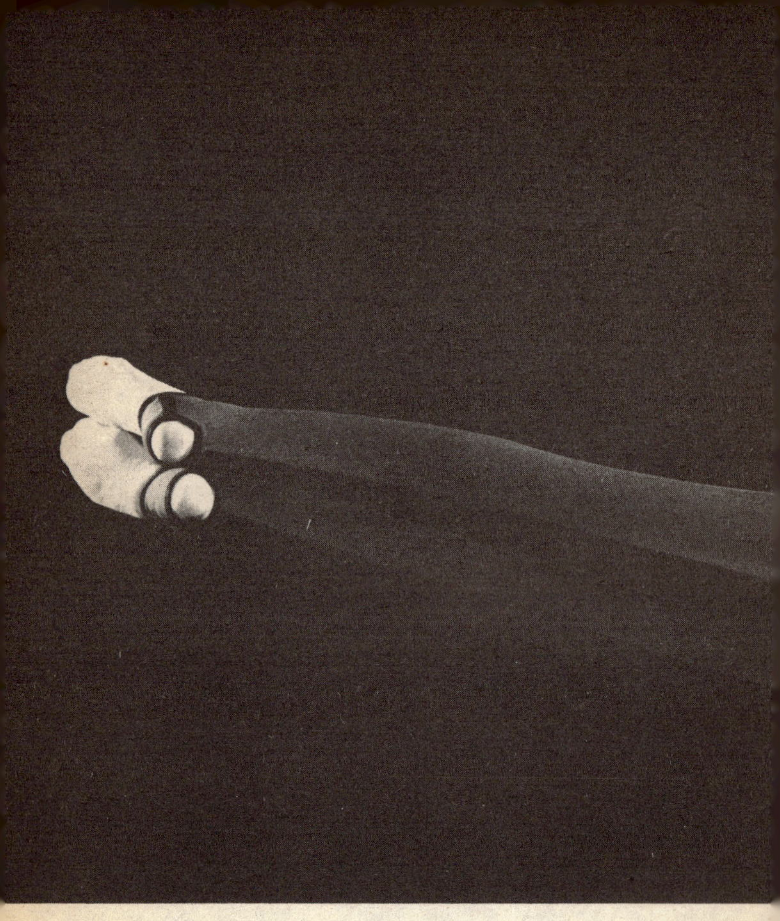

FIG. 136—*Perform the identical movements lying on your right side.*

FIG. 136

BACK PUSH-UP

Continued from Exercise #14, page 62

Practice Information

Perform the moderate raise of Fig. 43 once. Hold for 10. Perform the extreme raise twice. Hold each for 15.

FIG. 137—*Refer to Figs. 42 and 43. Now we attempt the highest raise possible. As the trunk is raised, place the top of the head on the floor. Continue to push up as high as possible. Knees must remain together. Hold your extreme position for 15.*

Slowly lower your trunk to the floor and return head to the normal position. Repeat.

FIG. 137

KNEE and THIGH STRETCH

Continued from Exercise #15, page 64

Practice Information

Perform once in the moderate position of Fig. 45. Hold for 10. Perform twice in your extreme position. Hold each for 15.

FIG. 138—*Refer to Figs. 44 and 45. We now attempt to lower knees to the floor. Pull up firmly on your feet, lower knees as far as possible. Keep spine erect. Hold for 15.* Feel *the thighs stretching.*

Allow your knees to return to the position of Fig. 44. Repeat.

FIG. 138

TWIST

Continued from Exercise #16, page 66

These movements provide a much more intensive stretch than those of the modified Twist we have been practicing. However, the principle remains the same: the manipulation of the spine in a "corkscrew" fashion for the immediate loosening of the entire back.

Important

Because of the number of separate movements that are required, this exercise is the most complicated of the study. Make certain you do not confuse "right" with "left." In Fig. 144 your head must be turned far to the right, otherwise you will not perform the complete twist.

Practice Information

When you learn this exercise there is no further need for the previous modified Twist.

Perform twice to the right side, then twice to the left side. Hold each twist for 20. Remember to concentrate on all movements and to *feel* the stretch in the extreme position.

FIG. 139

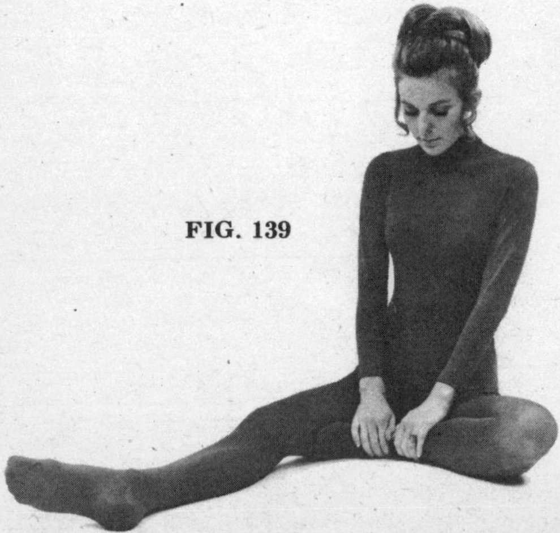

FIG. 139—*Sit with your legs outstretched. Take hold of your left foot and place it as illustrated. Heel is drawn in as far as possible.*

FIG. 140—*Bring your right foot in and take hold of the ankle.*

FIG. 140

FIG. 141

FIG. 141—*Swing the right leg over the left knee. Place the sole of the right foot firmly on the floor.*

FIG. 142—*Place your right hand firmly on the floor behind you. This is for balance.*

FIG. 143—*Now bring your left arm* over *the right knee and take a firm hold on your left knee. This movement locks the lumbar area.*

FIG. 144—*We are now able to twist the thoracic and cervical vertebrae against the lumbar lock. Slowly turn your trunk and head as far to your* right *as possible. Chin is close to shoulder. Trunk is held erect. Hold without motion for 20.* Feel *the twist.*

Slowly turn frontward and relax your trunk but retain your hold on the knee (Fig. 143). Rest a moment and repeat.

Slowly turn frontward, stretch your legs outward.

FIG. 142

FIG. 143

FIG. 144

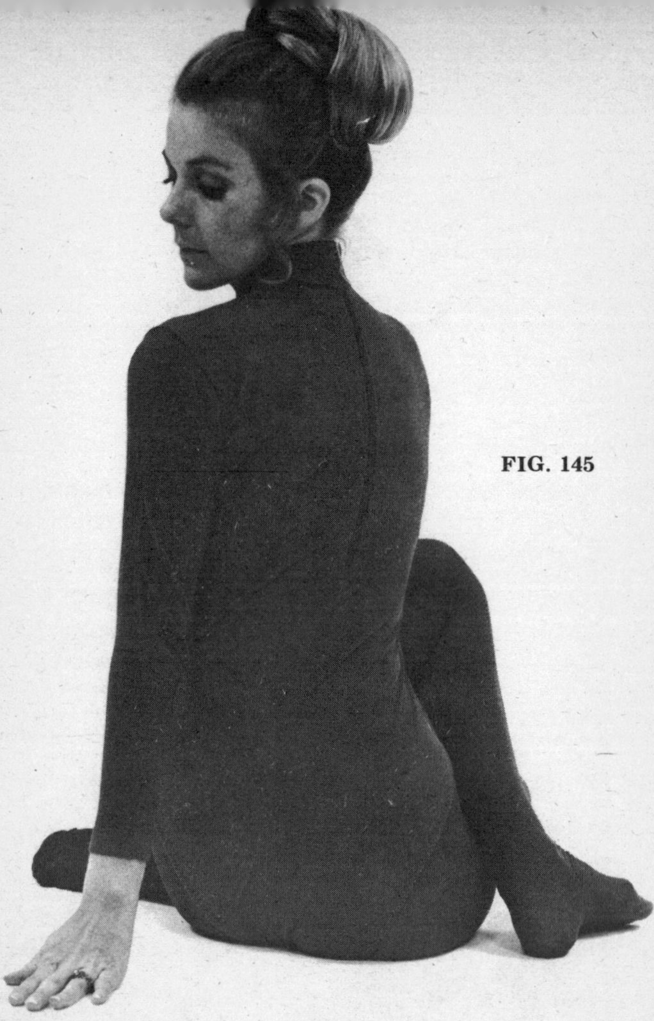

FIG. 145

FIG. 145—*Repeat the identical movements to the* left *side. Exchange the words "right" and "left" in the above directions. Fig. 145 depicts a back view of the completed twist to the left side. Hold for 20.*

Slowly turn frontward, rest a moment and repeat.

Following the final repetition, stretch your legs outward and relax.

LEG CLASP

Continued from Exercise #17, page 69

Practice Information

Perform once each in the knee, calf and ankle position. If the ankle position is too extreme, perform twice in the calf position. Hold each stretch for 10.

FIG. 146—*Refer to Figs. 50 and 51. Now clasp your hands behind your calves. Pull against the calves and draw trunk down as far as possible. Hold your extreme position for 10.* Feel *the stretch of the back and legs.*

Raise your trunk several inches and relax for a moment, but retain the clasp.

FIG. 146

FIG. 147

FIG. 147—*This is the advanced position that you will have to work into slowly and cautiously. Slide your clasped hands down from the calves to the ankles. Draw trunk down as far as possible. Hold your extreme position for 10. Again,* feel *the stretch.*

Unclasp the hands and very slowly straighten to the upright position. Relax.

RISHI'S POSTURE

Continued from Exercise #18, page 71

Practice Information

Perform once in the calf and once in the ankle positions. Hold each stretch for 10. Alternate the sides, left-right.

FIG. 148—*Refer to Figs. 52-56. Perform the movements of Figs. 52-54. Now the right hand moves down and holds the right ankle. Your left arm is behind you and the gaze follows the left hand.*

FIG. 148

FIG. 149—*The completed posture. Your left arm has moved once again to the overhead position and your gaze is on the back of the left hand. Hold for 10.*

Slowly raise your trunk to the upright position and bring your arms into the position of Fig. 52.

Twist to the right *and perform the identical movements holding the* left *ankle.* Feel *the stretch.*

Slowly straighten to the upright position of Fig. 52 (hands meet in front at eye level). Slowly lower arms to the sides and relax.

BALANCE POSTURE

Continued from Exercise #20, page 79

Practice Information

These are advanced balance postures and patient practice will bring success. If you lose your balance, pause a moment and begin again. Do not become discouraged and never laugh at yourself.

Perform the position of Fig. 150, followed by the variation of Fig. 152 twice on each side. Hold each position for 10. Alternate the sides, right arm raised—left arm raised; repeat.

FIG. 150—*Refer to Figs. 60-62. Here, we attempt to raise the left leg several inches farther (compare with Fig. 62). Remember to drop the head backward and look upward. Hold as steady as possible for 10. Focus your full attention on the point of balance.*

FIG. 150

FIG. 151

FIG. 152

FIG. 151—*This is a variation that is attempted when you are secure in the position of Fig. 150. Begin to push up and back with the left foot and lower the right arm as illustrated.*

FIG. 152—*The completed "frozen running" posture. The foot and leg are now as far up and back as possible and the arm is lowered to the position illustrated. Hold as steady as possible for 10.*

Slowly lower the arm to the side and the foot to the floor.

Perform the identical movements with the left arm raised.

ABDOMINAL EXERCISE (LIFTS)

Continued from Exercise #21, page 84

Important

It is necessary to catch on to the knack of executing the movements *while the breath is exhaled*. All air must be expelled and kept out in order to create a vacuum or you will not be able to lift sufficiently to form the large "hollow." We can further describe this movement as a "sucking in" of the abdomen—inward and upward. Imagine that you are attempting to breathe very deeply from the abdominal area. No air actually enters your lungs but the abdominal area goes through the motions of this deep breath during which it is sucked inward and upward.

Practice Information

Once the lifting technique is mastered, there is no further need for the contractions. The lifts are much more beneficial.

Perform five lifting and snapping out movements to *each exhalation*. Do five rounds in the Sitting, Standing and All-Fours positions so that you execute 25 movements in each position or 75 movements in all. Rest briefly between each group. An even rhythm, not speed, is important. Each lift is held for 2. There is no pause between the snapping out and the next lift.

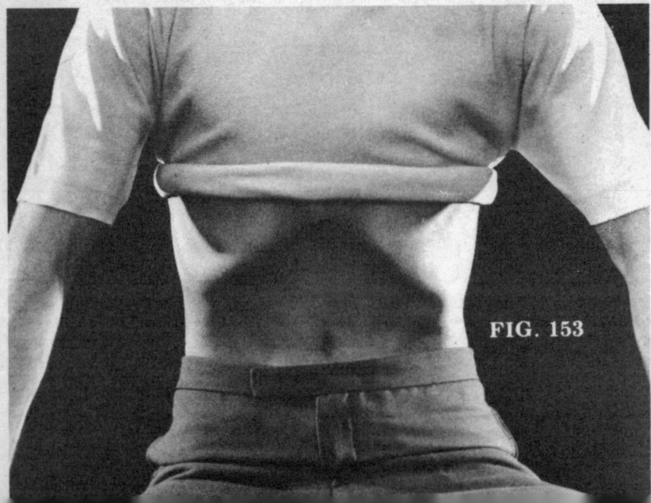

FIG. 153

FIG. 154

FIG. 153—*Refer to Figs. 63-65. Now we attempt not only to "contract" the abdomen but to "lift" it. Compare Fig. 153 with 64. It is essential to understand that this lifting movement can be successfully accomplished only if all air is* completely exhaled *from your lungs and no air is allowed to enter while the movements are performed.*

Exhale deeply and attempt to lift the abdomen as illustrated. No air can enter your lungs. Hold the lift for a count of two.

"Snap" the abdomen out as previously practiced.

Without pause repeat the lifting and snapping out.

FIG. 154—*Refer to Fig. 66. Perform the lifting movements in the standing position.*

FIG. 155—*Refer to Fig. 67. Perform the lifting movements in the All-Fours position.*

ALTERNATE LEG STRETCH

Continued from Exercise #22, page 90

Practice Information

Perform the calf, ankle, foot and advanced positions once each. Hold the calf and ankle positions for 10 and the foot and advanced position for 15. Do the movements with the left leg first, then the right. Keep your mind on the movements.

FIG. 156—*Refer to Figs. 68-73. Raise your arms as previously and bend backward as far as possible.*

FIG. 156

FIG. 157

FIG. 157—*Come forward slowly. Do the "rocking" movements we performed with the Back Stretch to loosen your spine.*

Take a firm hold on your left foot.

FIG. 158—*Pull your trunk down and rest your forehead on your left knee. Hold for 15.* Feel *the stretch throughout the leg.*

FIG. 159—*This is the advanced position that provides the maximum stretch for the leg and should be attempted only after you are comfortable in the position of Fig. 158. Lower both elbows to touch the floor. Hold for 15.* Feel *the intensive stretching.*

Very slowly raise your trunk to the upright position.

Extend your right leg. Rest hands on knees and relax a few moments.

Bring the left foot in and perform the identical movements with the right *leg extended.*

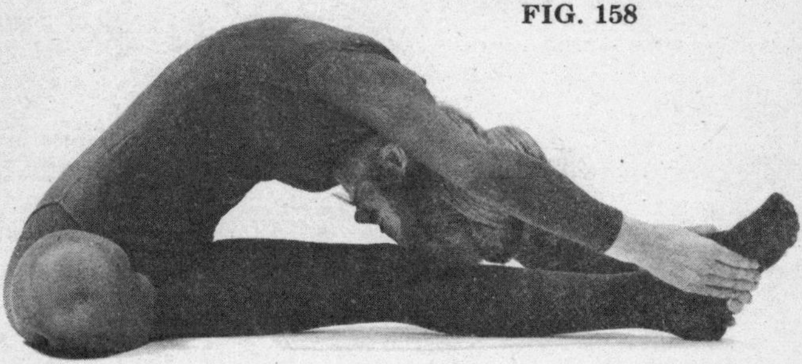

FIG. 158

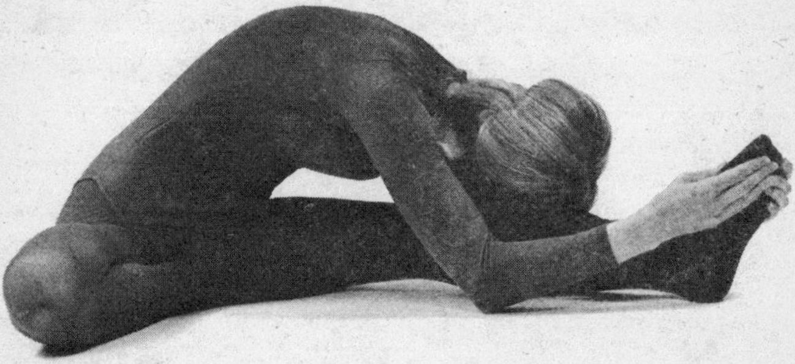

FIG. 159

PLOUGH

Continued from Exercise #24, page 97

Practice Information

Perform each of the three positions (Figs. 79, 160, 161) once. Hold each for 20.

FIG. 160—*Refer to Figs. 77-79. This position follows directly that of Fig. 79. Bring your arms up from the sides and clasp them on top of your head.*

You will now be able to inch back a short (but very significant) distance farther with your toes. Experience *the pressure moving from your lower back (where it was in Fig. 79) to the middle area. Hold for 20. Breathe as slowly as possible.*

FIG. 161—*In this advanced position we lower the knees to either side of the head and have them touch the floor if possible.* Experience *the pressure shifting from the middle area to the cervical. Hold for 20. Again, breathe as slowly as possible.*

Come out of the posture smoothly and gracefully, exactly as directed under Fig. 79.

FIG. 160

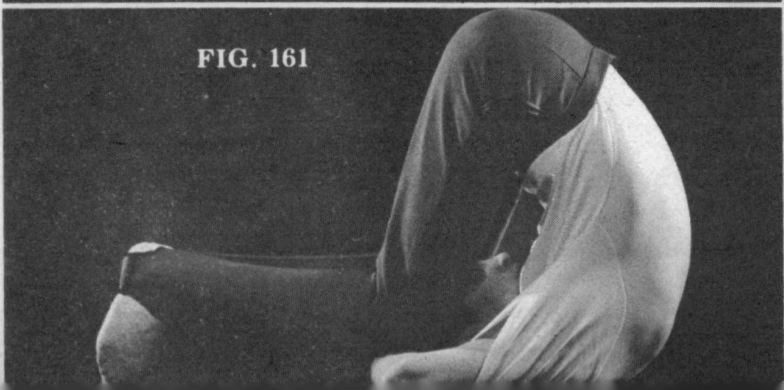

FIG. 161

HEAD STAND

Continued from Exercise #25, page 100

Practice Information

You can see that the objective of the instructions below is to have you feel completely secure in each of the intermediate positions between the Modified and Completed postures.

Hold the Modified and each of the intermediate positions for a count of 10. Remain in the completed posture for up to three minutes. Place a clock to the side of your head where you are able to time your extreme position. Add the seconds very gradually to the completed Head Stand; you can allow yourself to achieve the three-minute hold over a period of several months. There is no rush.

Many students perform a Modified Head Stand upon arising to effect a quicker awakening of the brain.

In the completed posture breathe slowly and fix your consciousness on the breathing. Try not to let the mind wander.

FIGS. 162-163—*Refer to Figs. 80-84. These positions follow directly the Modified posture of Fig. 84. Begin to straighten the legs. Remain in each of these positions for a count of 10 to make certain that you are secure and well balanced.* If you are shaky, do not continue *upward. Practice to attain steadiness here before going on.*

FIG. 162

FIG. 163

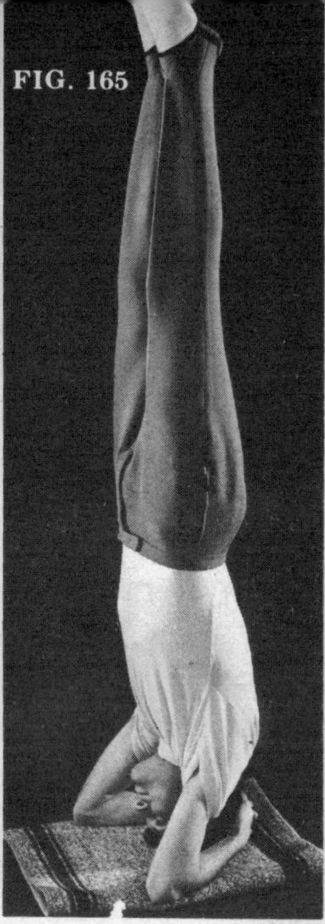

FIG. 164—*Note the position of the back and that the legs remain close together. Again, hold this for a count of 10. If you are unsteady, do not attempt the completed posture. Remain for the count of 10 (or less), lower the legs to the floor and try again tomorrow. If you feel secure, continue.*

FIG. 165—*The completed posture. The entire body is as straight as possible. Begin with a count of approximately 10 seconds and add a few seconds each practice session until three minutes are reached.*

Come out of the posture smoothly and gracefully by lowering your knees slowly to your chest and then lowering your feet to the floor. Try not to have the feet "bang" against the floor.

Remain with your head down for approximately one minute.

ALTERNATE NOSTRIL BREATHING

Continued from Exercise #26, page 106

It is suggested that the student practice with the elementary technique for at least one month and become completely adept in that breathing rhythm before undertaking this more advanced technique.

Important

You will see that you must now inhale more quickly and retain longer than before. In addition you must *suspend at the end of each exhalation.* Practice to make this routine very smooth; the breath must not "hiss" in the nostrils and the rhythm should become exact. Complete concentration on the counting is required.

Practice Information

Perform five rounds.

Refer to Figs. 85-88.

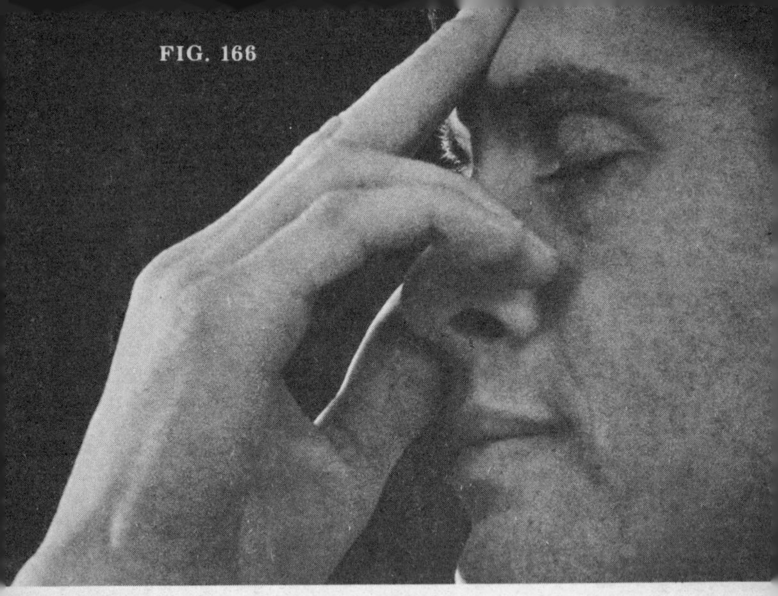

FIG. 166 — *We are now concerned with* an alteration of the breathing rhythm. *Also, we will include one additional step: The breath will be* suspended at the end of the exhalation, *as well as retained at the end of the inhalation.*

The new ratio of the breathing rhythm is: 1-4-2-1 and this ratio is translated into actual counting as follows:

exhale deeply through both nostrils	
inhale through the left	*— count 4*
close both nostrils and retain	*— count 16*
exhale through the right	*— count 8*
suspend (both nostrils closed, air held out of the lungs, no breathing)	*— count 4*
inhale through the right	*— count 4*
close both nostrils and retain	*— count 16*
exhale through the left	*— count 8*
suspend	*— count 4*
inhale through the left, etc.	*— count 4*

DAILY PRACTICE ROUTINES

The exercises we are learning in this book are too numerous to be used in their entirety during any one practice session. Therefore, we will divide the 31 techniques into three groups and use these groups in a rotating plan for successive days of practice. For example, Monday—Group A, Tuesday—Group B, Wednesday—Group C, Thursday—Group A, etc. It is important to keep track of your practice schedule so that in the event you are unable to exercise for one or more days, you can resume at the point where you left off.

You may follow this schedule regardless of how far you have progressed into the Intermediate Section. Simply perform your extreme position of the exercise called for whether this be from the Elementary or Intermediate Section. Naturally, as you progress you will be including more and more positions from the Intermediate Section. Each of the three routines should require approximately 20 to 30 minutes.

If you are working on a particular problem (weight, firming, tension, etc.) you can give extra attention to the exercises for this problem as listed in the "Special Problems" pages that follow. However, these should be practiced *in addition* to the regular routine of that day.

It is important not to perpetuate any incorrect patterns of movement; therefore, if at any time you have the slightest doubt regarding the correct execution of any of the movements, make certain to refer to the directions for the exercise in question. No posture is to be neglected, regardless of how difficult it may seem in the beginning stages. Each asana is essential in our study.

Be very accurate in your counting of the "holds" and "repetitions."

Remember also that certain individual exercises, including the Cobra, Head Stand, Complete Breath and Alternate Nostril Breathing, have been suggested for use whenever needed.

These routines will serve as a lifetime guide to your physical, emotional and mental well-being.

DAILY PRACTICE PLAN
(By Groups)

The figures in the parenthesis refer to the pages of both the Elementary and Intermediate sections where the exercise is instructed.

Group A

Deep Relaxation Posture (14)
Complete Breath (21)
— in cross-legged posture
Scalp Exercise (114)
Lion (116)
Neck Exercise (119)
Posture Exercise (121)
Bust Exercise (123)
Rishi's Posture (71, 171)
Abdominal Lifts (84, 176)
— in three positions
Knee and Thigh Stretch (64, 163)
Alternate Leg Stretch (90, 179)
Leg Over (95)
Back Push-Up (62, 162)
Locust (37, 142)
Head Stand (100, 183)
Alternate Nostril Breathing (106, 185)
— in cross-legged posture

Group B

Deep Relaxation Posture (14)
Complete Breath (21)
Scalp Exercise (114)
Lion (116)
Neck Exercise (119)
Posture Exercise (121)
Bust Exercise (123)
Chest Expansion (30, 134)
Triangle (47, 150)
Leg Clasp (69, 169)
Back Stretch (25, 131)
Twist (66, 164)
Bow (40, 144)
Shoulder Stand (54, 156)
Alternate Nostril Breathing (106, 185)

Group C

Deep Relaxation Posture (14)
Complete Breath (21)
Scalp Exercise (114)
Lion (116)
Neck Exercise (119)
Posture Exercise (121)
Bust Exercise (123)
Side Bend (43, 148)
Dancer's Posture (76)
Balance Posture (79, 173)
Abdominal Lifts (84, 176)
Backward Bend (50, 153)
Cobra (34, 138)
Side Raise (59, 159)
Plough (97, 182)
Alternate Nostril Breathing (106, 185)

SPECIAL PROBLEMS INDEX

The following tables list the exercises to which you can devote special attention if you are attempting to overcome a particular problem. The exercise pages are indicated in the parentheses. These suggestions are offered from the Yogic viewpoint and are not to be used as a substitute for medical treatment. If you are in doubt regarding the effect of any of the postures, consult your physician.

Backward Bend (50, 153)
Shoulder Stand (54, 156)
Head Stand (100, 183)
Plough (97, 182)
Back Push-Up (62, 162)

Nervous System (general tension & insomnia relieved)

Deep Relaxation Posture (14)
Complete Breath (21)
Alternate Nostril Breathing (106, 185)
Neck Exercise (119)
Cobra (34, 138)
Shoulder Stand (54, 156)
Chest Expansion (30, 134)

Posture (improved)

Chest Expansion (30, 134)
Backward Bend (50, 153)
Posture Exercise (121)
Bust Exercise (123)
Bow (40, 144)
Cobra (34, 138)

Scalp (promoting healthy condition of; reduce falling hair, improve color and lustre)

Scalp Exercise (114)
Shoulder Stand (54, 156)
Head Stand (100, 183)
Backward Bend (50, 153)
Plough (97, 182)

Spine (adjusting vertebrae, removing stiffness, strengthening)

Chest Expansion (30, 134)
Cobra (34, 138)
Bow (40, 144)
Plough (97, 182)
Back Stretch (25, 131)
Rishi's Posture (71, 171)
Leg Clasp (69, 169)
Twist (66, 164)
Backward Bend (50, 153)

Weight (in conjunction with correct diet)

Reduced in waist and hips:

Abdominal Exercise (84, 176)
Shoulder Stand (54, 156)
Plough (97, 182)
Side Bend (43, 148)
Twist (66, 164)
Leg Over (95)

Reduced in buttocks, thighs and calves:

Shoulder Stand (54, 156)
Cobra (34, 138)
Locust (37, 142)
Bow (40, 144)
Side Raise (59, 159)
Back Push-Up (62, 162)
Triangle (47, 150)
Dancer's Posture (76)

YOGA FOR HEALTH.

Mr. Hittleman's television series may be seen in many areas. For a free newsletter and catalog containing the author's other publications, write to:
Richard Hittleman,
P.O. Box 554
Santa Cruz, California 95061